PREFACE

Plautus wrote upwards of fifty plays, of which twenty have survived more or less in their entirety.[1] In making my choice for this anthology, I tried not only to include his best but to give some idea of his range. His forte was farce, and my selections exemplify at least two of his favorite farcical devices: mistaken identity (*Amphitryon*) and the lecherous old codger (*Casina*). *The Pot of Gold* reveals what Plautus could do with the subtler humor to be evoked from character.

I have arranged the plays alphabetically by their Latin titles (*Amphitryo, Aulularia, Casina*), as is traditional in editions of Plautus. In spite of many learned attempts, no one has yet succeeded in demonstrating convincingly the chronological order of his work (see p. xii).

In these translations I have followed the same principles I did in my *Masters of Ancient Comedy*, and I can do no better than repeat what I wrote there (p. viii) to explain what my procedure has been:

"All Greek and Roman drama was in verse. Moreover, . . . Plautus [was], in a sense, writing musical comedy: a considerable portion of [his] plays is not dialogue to be spoken but lyrics to be sung. These by their very nature called for translation in verse. Everywhere else I have used prose.

[1] I say "more or less" because all but one of the preserved manuscripts of his work derive from a single manuscript of the eighth century A.D. which was, unfortunately, in a mutilated condition, and, as a consequence, there are gaps in the text that range from a few lines (see, e.g., *Casina*, ll. 889, 890) to whole scenes (see, e.g., *Amphitryon*, l. 1035).

"The usual purpose of a verse translation is to retain the style and spirit of the original at the expense, if necessary, of literal accuracy; and, of a prose translation, precisely the opposite. What I have done is to reverse this usual state of affairs: I have chosen prose in order to retain the spirit, if not the style, of the original, and my prose is, if anything, more free than many a translation in verse.

"There have been many periods in the history of drama when verse was the only accepted vehicle for comedy. Today, of course, playwrights writing in the vein of . . . Plautus use normal colloquial speech. My aim was to make these ancient plays sound as much like contemporary comedy as I could—and still remain a translator and not an adapter. That meant not only using prose, but prose that reflected the vocabulary and rhythms of contemporary speech. Every line I translated I subjected to a simple test: I read it aloud and asked myself whether it sounded the way a person would express himself in the given situation today. Frequently the original lent itself to a rendering that satisfied this requirement and was at the same time a close translation; more often, close translation was impossible and I rendered the general sense of a passage with no attempt to reproduce the meaning of the individual words; at times I frankly paraphrased. All references that would make sense only to ancient audiences or modern scholars I replaced with some sort of current equivalent. For the ubiquitous oaths and exclamations that invoke the names of ancient deities I substituted modern expressions; I converted drachmas and talents into dollars (allowing for current inflation has made my figures considerably higher than those in earlier translations); I replaced ancient geographical names with modern equivalents; I doctored the jokes where necessary to make them intelligible to today's audiences. Moreover, in line with my aim to make living theater of these plays, I added full stage directions, just as a modern playwright would."

The lyric portions of the originals are extremely fluid and flexible, characterized by lines of unequal length and by frequent changes of meter. My renderings reproduce only the

Amphitryon

AND

Two Other Plays

By Plautus

Edited and Translated by LIONEL CASSON

W · W · NORTON & COMPANY

New York · London

To Bill *and* Bette

This book was previously published as part of a volume entitled *Six Plays of Plautus*. The companion volume, *"The Menaechmus Twins" and Two Other Plays,* is also available in Norton paperback.

First published in Norton paperback 1971 by arrangement with Doubleday & Company, Inc.

ISBN: 978-0-393-00601-8

W. W. Norton & Company, Inc., 500 Fifth Avenue, New York, N.Y. 10110
http://www.wwnorton.com

W. W. Norton & Company Ltd., Castle House, 75/76 Wells Street, London W1T 3QT

PRINTED IN THE UNITED STATES OF AMERICA

4 5 6 7 8 9 0

metrical pace, as it were. Where the mood was comic, I used rhymed verse; where more serious, unrhymed.

Plautus chose the names he assigned his characters with great care. A number are not actually names but pure comic inventions, and for these I used English equivalents (e.g., Grape, the old hag of a servant in *The Pot of Gold*, is in the original *Staphyla* "cluster of grapes"). For other characters, he (or the author of the Greek original he adapted) used common Greek names which were somehow especially apt, just as a playwright of today will emphasize a female character's nature by giving her a name such as Faith or Grace; in these cases I kept the original name but explained its aptness in the stage directions.

Plautus wrote his plays to be performed without breaks. Subsequently, editors introduced act divisions. Since these have become traditional, and serve a useful purpose as well, I have retained them.

As always, I owe a large debt of gratitude to my most careful and helpful critic, my father. The introduction and stage directions have everywhere benefited from his rigorous insistence on accuracy in language, and the dialogue from his keen ear for accuracy in idiom. My wife contributed many a well-turned phrase and gave brightness to many a lackluster line. And I am grateful to the John Simon Guggenheim Memorial Foundation for providing in an indirect way the free time that made this volume possible—in an indirect way because these translations were largely done as daily relaxation after hours of close research on the topic for which I had actually received my fellowship.

Lionel Casson

Rome
September 1962

CONTENTS

INTRODUCTION

Sometime around 250 B.C., in the tiny mountain village of Sarsina high in the Apennines of Umbria, ancient Rome's best-known playwright was born.

We know so little about his life that we're not even sure of his full name; probably—but only probably—it was Titus Maccius Plautus. We can only guess how a backwoods country boy managed to leave his village, to learn Latin so well he achieved effects with it no later writers ever matched (the native tongue of Sarsina was not Latin but Umbrian, a relative of Latin), to learn the literary language of the day, Greek (see below, p. xvii), to crack the world of the theater at the capital, and through it to fight his way to reputation and money. According to one of the stories told about him years after he died, he got his start in the theater as an actor in native farces. This could very well be true: Plautus' plays show unmistakably that their author knew what went on behind the stage as well as on it. Moreover, what easier way was there for a boy with the appropriate talent to escape the shackles of a small town than by joining an itinerant theatrical troupe? Once Plautus achieved fame, he never lost it: when he died, in 184 B.C., he was the dean of Rome's writers of comedy.

Comedy itself was only three centuries or so older than he was. It had achieved definite form where so much else of Western culture had, in Athens of the fifth century B.C.: the first recorded performance of a comedy took place in March 486 B.C., in the Theater of Dionysus on the south slope of Athens' Acropolis.

But the type of comedy that flourished in fifth-century Athens, Greek "Old Comedy" as it has been called, neither lasted very long nor started any important trends. When its best-known exponent, Aristophanes, died, it more or less died with him. Old Comedy was, essentially, topical satire, and Aristophanes' plays, full of withering, uproarious jibes at contemporary Athenian politics and politicos, education and educators, writings and writers, did not interest subsequent generations to whom all this was just so much ancient history, and whose taste in comedy ran in different directions.

Toward the end of his life, however, Aristophanes started to mine a comic vein that, being more universal in appeal, lasted a good deal longer, right through Plautus down to our own times, in fact. He shifted the emphasis from satire to humor, and began to write about people as a class, not specific personalities, and to poke fun at men's ways in general, not at their behavior as citizens in a given place at a given time.

By 300 B.C., this form of comedy, Greek "New Comedy" as it has been called, had come to maturity and was providing the principal and preferred theatrical fare of the day. Aristophanes was a thing of the past; audiences jammed the theaters to see the latest works of the masters of New Comedy, of Diphilus, Philemon, Apollodorus of Carystus, and, above all, Menander. They wrote about ordinary people, mocking—Menander gently, the others more boisterously— human foibles and crotchets, the laughable things people are prone to do, the silly behavior certain circumstances almost invariably call forth. The world these playwrights chose to portray is small: they deal almost exclusively with the doings of upper middle-class households. The dramatis personae are equally limited: the father of the household, irascible or stupid as plot requires; his formidable wife; their idler of a son; scheming servants; dull-witted servants; longwinded cooks; gold-digging courtesans; famished hangers-on; flint-hearted pimps. The plot often revolves about, or at the very least includes, a love affair, and there was an unfortunate tendency (we haven't overcome it to this day) to tell—with variations, to be sure—the story of the boy who meets the girl, can't marry her because she has no money or comes from the wrong side of the tracks, but ends up living happily ever after since she turns out to be the rich neighbor's long-lost daughter.

According to the ancient critics, Menander and the other great names in Greek New Comedy wrote consummate masterpieces. We today are in no position either to confirm or contest this judgment for, of the hundreds of these works that were staged, all that has survived is one complete play and that a rather poor specimen, half of another, and one third each of two more.[1]

New Comedy was immensely popular. The latest productions of Diphilus and Menander, after opening in Athens, went to theaters all over the Greek-speaking world, in Asia Minor, on the Aegean Isles, along the coast of North Africa, and—most important for comedy's subsequent history—in South Italy.

As early as 700 B.C., the lower part of Italy, from Naples south through Sicily, had been largely taken over by Greeks. The area was dotted with their populous and well-to-do cities, each of which by 300 B.C. had its theater where not only local farces and skits were put on but also the latest imports of New Comedy from Athens.

To the north lay Rome. Until just a few decades before Plautus was born, Rome was relatively obscure and provincial, with no pretensions to culture, a nation of hard-fisted farmers and hard-fighting soldiers. However, by the time Plautus was an adult, she had extended her power southward and was the acknowledged mistress of the Greek cities of southern Italy. Her soldiers, statesmen, and merchants came into contact with, and got eye-filling glimpses of, a new, far more sophisticated and gracious way of life. Among other things, they were exposed to the delights of the Greek stage

[1] For translations of these, see my *Masters of Ancient Comedy*, pp. 65–175.

and, in no time at all, developed a healthy appetite for it. This was a milestone in the history of comedy: it was responsible for the creation of Latin comedy, and Latin comedy is the direct ancestor of much of the comedy of later Western literature.

The Romans, to be sure, had some theatrical fare of their own. Their village fiestas featured several types of short, boisterous farce, including one in which song and dance played an important part; if Plautus actually did start his career as an actor, it must have been in pieces of this kind. But it was all rather primitive stuff. In 240 B.C., a Greek named Livius Andronicus translated and adapted a Greek New Comedy for a Roman audience and immediately started a vogue; he had filled a need. Latin versions of Greek plays quickly found a place on programs alongside the local fare, and, in larger communities, easily outstripped it in popularity. Livius was followed by Gnaeus Naevius (ca. 270–201 B.C.), Rome's first native playwright, who, in addition to adapting Greek works, inaugurated true Roman comedy by writing original plays in Latin. He apparently was a talented author, but unfortunately only fragments of his work have been preserved. The distinction of having produced the earliest Latin plays to survive goes to his gifted younger contemporary, Plautus.

Plautus, in a very real sense, faced the same problems as a writer for Broadway today. He had to turn out pieces that would please a motley, more or less undiscriminating audience, and he had to sell them to tough, business-minded producers.

In the ancient world, plays were put on as part of the general entertainment given at public festivals. During Plautus' lifetime, Rome had four great annual festivals whose programs included drama, and special events such as the funerals of great men or victory celebrations provided still further opportunities for the playwright. Plays were never lone features on these occasions; they shared the program with chariot races, horse races, boxing matches, and other similar entertainments. The theatrical troupes, small groups of five or six actors usually of Greek extraction, were managed by a *dominus gregis* or "leader of the troupe." He was producer and director combined: he entered into a contract with the officials in charge of a given festival to supply a certain number of performances, and, when the time came, staged them. The officials payed him a lump sum and furnished the facilities: for the actors a temporary wooden structure which was nothing more than a long, low, narrow stage with a backdrop showing two or three house fronts, and for the audience temporary wooden bleachers. It was the job of the *dominus* to find his troupe likely scripts, which he either bought himself or recommended for purchase to the officials.

These were the men Plautus had to deal with: the *domini*, the festival officials, and on occasion a Roman aristocrat who was footing the bill for a special event. For one reason above all others he had no trouble peddling his plays: he knew what his audiences wanted, and he gave it to them.

Plautus as a playwright is not original in the strictest sense. In writing a play, he began, following in the footsteps of Livius, with a Greek original, a work by one of the writers of New Comedy. But he quickly parts company with Livius, who more or less faithfully rendered his originals into Latin. Since a close translation of a play by, for example, Menander would have little appeal for the crowds at a Roman festival, Plautus generally took from the Greek only the outline of the plot, the characters, and selected segments of the dialogue, and then stepped out on his own. In a sense he worked the way playwrights of today do when they convert a "legitimate" comedy into a musical. Along with revamping the dialogue, he replaced the relatively simple metrical pattern of the original with one more complex and, perhaps as a carry-over from his youthful days as an actor in native farce, introduced frequent scenes in song and dance (the music and dance that accompanied these have disappeared without trace; we are left with only the bare lyrics). Furthermore, since he was writing not for intellectuals but for the people who patronized sporting events and circuses, and since his listeners were there to be amused, he did his level best to make them laugh from the belly. Without a second thought he would interrupt the flow of the action for a scene of pure slapstick or for a series of lowbrow jokes; he made up broadly comic names to label his characters; he explained every turn of the plot to make sure the slowest wits could follow it; he even explained the jokes to make sure everyone got them. At all costs he kept the pot of the action boiling, the stream of gags and puns and comic alliterations flowing. It is of no avail to find fault with him for not providing real endings for his plays, for introducing characters and then abruptly dropping them, for making, in a word, the most elementary blunders in playwrighting. He did not care—the play was not the thing, the laughs were.

None of the Greek plays he adapted has survived, and we consequently cannot be certain of the exact extent of his changes, but there cannot be much doubt that they were far-reaching. A given play by Plautus very likely has much less in common with the work from which it was taken than, say, *My Fair Lady* has with Shaw's *Pygmalion*.

Much scholarly effort has been expended in trying to work out the chronological order of Plautus' comedies and thereby trace his development as a playwright, but without much success. However, we can be fairly certain that the three included here belong to his mature years. The *Casina* was perhaps one of his latest works; it seems pretty clear that, as Plautus grew older, he tended to increase the length of the lyric portions, and of all his plays the *Casina* has the largest proportion of these.

Plautus has been as popular after death as he was during his lifetime. If he owes a debt to his Greek predecessors, later playwrights of the highest stature have evened the account by being indebted to him, from Shakespeare in the sixteenth century (*The Comedy of Errors* is based on *The Menaechmus Twins*) through Molière in the seventeenth (e.g., *l'Avare* is based on *The Pot of Gold*) to Giraudoux in the twentieth (*Amphitryon 38* is an adaptation of the *Amphitryon*). Along with his younger contemporary, Terence, Plautus kept the spirit of Greek New Comedy alive and enabled it to make its great contributions to later literature. Dickens' Sam Weller, Wodehouse's Jeeves, the girls in the movies who come from the wrong side of the tracks and then turn out to be the long-lost daughters of eminently eligible parents—these and countless others are the lineal descendants of Pseudolus, Trachalio, Palaestra, and others of Plautus' dramatis personae. Nor is he merely a disembodied literary influence; he is still living theater. *A Funny Thing Happened on the Way to the Forum*, which was a success on Broadway some years ago, was a pastiche of *Pseudolus, Casina,* and others, and before that, the last of a long line of adaptations of *The Menaechmus Twins,* Richard Rodgers' and Lorenz Hart's *The Boys from Syracuse*, was a smash hit as a musical comedy and a motion picture. Probably no other single writer has had so profound and continuing an influence on the history of comedy.

BIBLIOGRAPHICAL NOTE

For anyone interested in studying further Plautus' plays and their influence, or any phase of Roman comedy, George Duckworth's monumental *The Nature of Roman Comedy* (Princeton University Press, 1952) provides a useful starting point. It covers, with extensive bibliography, just about every phase of the subject.

AMPHITRYON

DRAMATIS PERSONAE

MERCURY

SOSIA, *servant of Amphitryon (slave)*

JOVE

ALCMENA, *wife of Amphitryon*

AMPHITRYON, *Alcmena's husband, commander in chief of the Theban army*

BLEPHARO, *captain of Amphitryon's ship*

BROMIA, *maid of Alcmena (slave)*

[THESSALA, *maid of Alcmena (slave)*]

SCENE

In front of Amphitryon's house in Thebes.

PROLOGUE

(The door of Amphitryon's house opens, and a figure emerges, to all outward appearances a typical slave of the comic stage: short, slight, bearded, and with a countenance that reveals equal parts of wiliness and self-interest. Besides the standard servant's garb, he has on his head the broad-brimmed hat the Greeks wore against the sun when traveling. He walks downstage and addresses the audience.)

PROLOGUE Do you want me to be bighearted and see that your business transactions, all your buying and selling, make money? Do you want my help in general? Do you want me to expedite your business speculations, foreign and domestic, at present in operation or scheduled for the future, and have them produce steady, fat profits? Do you want me to see that you and all friends and relatives get only good news, and to deliver only messages that will best promote the public welfare? *(Importantly)* I hardly need remind you that the other gods have assigned *me* the responsibility for handling all messages and profits. *(Resuming his former tone)* So, if you want me to aid and abet the pouring of perennial profits into your pockets, please, all of you, don't make any noise during this performance and be fair and honest critics after it's over.

Now let me tell you who ordered me to come here and why, and at the same time give you my name: the orders come from Jove, and my name is Mercury. The reason my father's sent me here is to ask a favor of you. Of course, he's perfectly aware that you'll take whatever he tells you as an order, since he knows you respect and fear the name of Jove, as you should. Nevertheless, he specifically instructed me to put this to you as a request, in nice, polite language. *(Confidentially, gesturing toward the dressing room)* After all, the Jove who told me to come here is just as much afraid of getting into trouble as any of you: his mother was flesh and blood and so was his father, so it's

no wonder that he worries about his own skin. The same
goes for me: I'm Jove's son and, if he should get in trouble,
I'm afraid of catching the disease.

So, that being the case, I come to you in peace, and I
bring a peaceful message. The favor I want to ask is simple and perfectly proper: I'm here as a proper person to
put a proper request to proper people. After all, it's not
proper to ask for improper things from proper people, and
it's stupid to ask for proper things from improper people—
they're a criminal bunch who don't know what right is
and don't hold by it.

Now, please, all of you, pay attention to what I'm going
to say. Our wish should be your command—we deserve
this from you and the nation, Father and I. In tragedies
I've seen all the others—Father Neptune, Lady Virtue,
Lady Victory, Lord Mars, Lady War—reel off all the favors
they've done for you, but do I really have to give you a
list of the good that my father, King of Heaven, has de-
signed and constructed for all of you? And Father's never
been one to nag good people about the good he's done
them. He takes it for granted you're all grateful for it.

Now then, first I'll tell you the favor I've come here to
ask, and then I'll explain the plot of this tragedy. (*As if
taken aback*) What are these frowns for? (*As if a light has
suddenly dawned*) Because I said the play was going to
be a tragedy? (*Airily*) I'm a god—I'll have everything
changed. If you want, I'll turn it from a tragedy to a comedy
without altering a line. Well, do you want me to or not?
(*Suddenly grinning foolishly*) How stupid of me! I'm a
god! I know what you want, I understand your feelings in
the matter perfectly. I'll make it into a comedy with some
tragedy mixed in. After all, with kings and gods appearing
in it, I don't think it would be right to make it pure comedy. But, let's face it, a servant *does* play an important
part. So, as I said just before, I'll make it a tragicomedy.

But to get back to the favor Jove instructed me to ask of
you. He wants detectives to go through every seat in every
row of the house. If they spot a claque working for any

actor, they're to strip each offender of his coat, right here
in the house, and hold it as bail. (*Mimicking the manner
of a court clerk*) If anyone tries to fix the awarding of
prizes for the actors or other artists, either in writing or in
person or through third parties, or if the government officials in charge do the fixing themselves, Jove hereby rules
that the guilty parties be sentenced under the statute ap-
plicable had said parties been convicted of malfeasance
in seeking public office. (*Indignantly*) Victors survive
struggles through strength not sneakiness and subterfuge;
why shouldn't an actor be liable to the same legal penal-
ties as holders of our highest office? Men ought to compete
on the basis of character not claques. Good, honest performances will create their own claques—*if* the men who
do the judging are honest.

Here's another order I've received: detectives are to be
assigned to actors, too. Any actor who arranges for a
claque to applaud for himself, or who arranges to cut
down on a competitor's applause, is to get the whip till it
makes tatters of his hide along with his costume. Now, don't
be surprised that Jove is taking such good care of actors
today. Nothing to be surprised about: Jove himself is going
to act in this play. (*Pauses and looks over the whole audience*) What are you so surprised about? As if we're introducing anything new in having Jove on the stage! Why,
just last year, right in this theater, the actors prayed to
Jove, and he came down on stage to rescue them.[1] And
then, of course, he's always appearing in tragedy. So, as I
say, he'll act in the play today, and I will too. And now
your attention please, while I explain the plot of this
comedy.

(*Gesturing toward the backdrop*) The city here is
Thebes. (*Pointing to Amphitryon's house*) In that house
there, lives Amphitryon; he was actually born at Argos,
the son of a citizen of Argos. He's married to Alcmena,
King Electryon's daughter. At the moment Amphitryon is

---

[1] Apparently last year's play ended with a *deus ex machina*.

on active duty as commander in chief of the army, since
Thebes is at war with the Teleboans.

When Amphitryon went off to the front his wife was
pregnant. (*Grinning knowingly*) Now, I think you're all
aware by this time of the way my father carries on, the
liberties he allows himself in this sort of thing, what a
lover he can become once his affections have found an
object. He began carrying on an affair with Alcmena behind her husband's back. He borrowed her husband's looks
for himself, made love to her, and made her pregnant on
his own. I want you to be sure to get Alcmena's situation
straight: she's pregnant by the both of them, by her husband and by almighty Jove. (*Gesturing toward the house*)
Father's inside there right now in bed with her. That's why
tonight's running longer than usual: it'll go on till he's had
his pleasure from where he wants it. He's doing all this, of
course, disguised to look like Amphitryon. Incidentally,
don't be surprised at this get-up I'm wearing, at the way
I've come here dressed like a servant. I'm introducing you
to an age-old story, but in a new garb—that's why I've
come here (*pointing to his costume*) in this new get-up.

All right. Father's inside there at this very moment; yes,
Jove himself right there. He's changed himself into the
image of Amphitryon, and all the servants who see him
think that that's who he is. (*Smiling*) He can be a real
quick-change artist when the spirit moves him. I've changed
myself to look like Sosia, Amphitryon's servant, who's off
at the front with his master. This way I can be Father's
servant during his affair, and the household won't want to
know who I am when they see me running around the
place all day. They'll think I'm a servant, one of themselves, and won't question who I am or what I'm here for.

(*Confidentially*) Father's inside now, (*rapturously*) loll-
ing in the lap of the lovely lady he loves. He's busy telling
Alcmena all about what happened to Amphitryon at the
front. There she is, in the arms of her seducer, and she
thinks she's with her husband! Right now he's telling her
how Amphitryon routed the enemy's troops and was given

a pile of presents as reward. (*As if telling a secret*) We've absconded with all the gifts he got out there. (*Airily*) Father can do whatever he wants to, with no trouble at all.

Now, today Amphitryon's coming home from the front along with the servant whose looks I'm using. (*Taking out a cluster of feathers and sticking them in his hat*) To make it easier for you to tell us apart, I'll always have these little feathers in my hat, while Father, under his hat, will have a little gold tassel, which Amphitryon won't have. None of the household here will be able to see these marks of identification, but you will.

(*His attention caught, looks toward the wings, stage right.*) There's Amphitryon's servant Sosia now, carrying a lantern. He's just come from the waterfront. As soon as he gets to the house, I'll drive him away. You pay attention: it'll be well worth your while to see Jove and Mercury do an act!

(*He steps back and hides in the shadows near the door of the house.*)

ACT I

(Enter Sosia carrying a lantern. He is the spitting image of the disguised Mercury except for the telltale feathers in the hat.)

SONG

SOSIA

For guts and nerve no man alive comes close to me right
now.

I'm walking alone this time of night though I know damned
well just how

Young kids carry on. Or the cops might see me and clap me
into jail.

And then next morning I'd be sprung—to report to the
whipping detail!

With no chance to plead my case in court, and the master
not around,

They'll all be absolutely convinced the case against me is
sound;

Eight bruisers then will make me an anvil and pound me
full of dents.

Arriving home from overseas, I'll be welcomed at public
expense!

(Shaking his head mournfully)

> The sweat my master was in! I had to go
> From the dock this time of night though I said no.

(Bitterly)

> He couldn't wait till day to send me from there!
> No easy job, this serving a millionaire;
> A rich man's servant leads a lousy life.
> All his nights and days it's just a constant strife
> To keep up with the errands and jobs he has to do,
> With never a moment's peace or rest for you.
> What wealthy master's done work himself? Not one!

So whatever a man can think up, he thinks can be
   done.
"It's all right," he thinks, and never thinks how long
The job may be. But whether the order's all *wrong*
And *not* all right, will never enter his mind.
So a slave runs into wrongs of every kind.
You have to sweat—and shrug and be resigned.

MERCURY (*to the audience*)

Hey, I'm the one who should complain that way!
Till Pappa pressed me into service today
I'd no idea what slavery meant.
Now, *he's* been used to being a slave
Since birth—and listen to him rave!

SOSIA (*working himself up*)

I'm a stupid slob of a slave, I am! I got the idea too soon
To pray to the gods on my safe return, and thank them for
   the boon.
If the gods should ever return the thanks in the way that I
   deserve,
They'd commission a guy to welcome my face as a private
   punching preserve.

(*Shaking his head bitterly*)

That safe return they blessed me with, like an ingrate I
   upset!

MERCURY (*to the audience*)

Not many are like this fellow here—he knows just what he
   should get.

SOSIA

No Theban thought, and neither did I, that things would
   turn out the way
They did turn out: that, safe and sound, we'd make it
   home one day.
Our conquering army's conquered the foe, and now we're
   home again;
A bitter battle's been fought and won, and all the enemy
   slain.

Our men by their morale and might have stormed and won
    the town

Of the nation that so often cruelly cut our people down.

We owe it most to Amphitryon, who led us like a wonder:

He's brought to all his countrymen new lands, renown,
    and plunder,

And Creon he's put upon the throne as king of Thebes for
    life.

Now me he's sent ahead from the dock to go home and
    tell his wife

How, by leading, guiding, ordering, her husband served
    the state.

(*Thoughtfully*)

Now, how to tell her once I'm there—just let me concentrate.

I can, of course, just think up lies, the way I usually do,

Since, when the fight was at its height, my running speed *Self-*
    was, too.   *mockery*

(*Shrugging*)

I'll simply pretend that I was there and tell her things I've
    heard.

But to figure a way to spin this yarn and think up every
    word

Is what I want to work out first.

(*After a moment's deep thought, brightly*)

                         I'll say that this occurred.

(*In a burlesque of the tragic stage, Sosia clears his throat
resoundingly, strikes a histrionic pose, and launches into a
dramatic recitative à la grand opera.*)

When we first arrived at the enemy's land, the minute we
    came ashore,

Amphitryon at once picked out the leaders on his staff,

And these he sent to the Teleboans to make his position
    clear:

If they were willing to come to terms and, avoiding vio-
    lence,

Would apprehend and deliver up the bandits with their
    booty,
Would give us back what they'd carried off, he'd start for
    home at once,
He'd lead his forces out of the land and leave the foe in
    peace.
But if they intended otherwise, and refused what he was
    asking,
Then with all the might and men he had, he'd attack and
    storm their town.
The delegates Amphitryon sent repeated this word for
    word.
The Teleboan people, though, brave men with confidence
In both their fighting spirit and strength, got very arrogant
And proceeded to tell our delegates off in no uncertain
    terms:
They answered that, when it came to war, they could well
    defend themselves,
So Thebes had better leave their land, get the army out,
    and fast.
The minute this word was brought to him, Amphitryon
    drew up
His whole great force in front of the camp; the enemy like-
    wise
Mobilized his men in front of the town, magnificently
    armed.

(*Working himself up*)

Once the armies were out in full force on each side,
All the men took their stations, the ranks were drawn up.
We deployed our platoons as we usually do,
And the enemy lined up his forces against us.
Then both the commanders, advancing into
No man's land, held a parley away from the ranks.
Whichever side lost in the fight, they agreed,
Would surrender their city, their temples, their fields,
Their houses, their hearths, their own bodies and souls.

Once agreed, they went back, and the trumpets blared
   forth.
The earth echoed the sound. From each side came a yell.
Each commander, both their man and ours, said his
   prayers
To great Jove, and exhorted his soldiers to fight.

(With great excitement)

In the struggle each man gave his all.
Swords clanged; lances broke; and the shouts
Of the men rose as high as the sky.
And an actual cloud floated up
From the breath given off as they gasped.
Scores of soldiers succumbed to their wounds.
Then at last, as we hoped for, our men
See that victory's coming their way.
More and more of the enemy fall.
In we charge to drive home the attack.
Like furies we fight—and they crack!

(Pauses, then resumes with great feeling)

Yet not one of the foe turned to flee from the field.
They kept standing their ground, never breaking the
   lines.
Sooner die than abandon their posts, was their thought.
Each fell where he stood; the very corpses kept ranks.

(Excitedly again)

When Amphitryon notices this,
He immediately orders a charge
Of his cavalry on the right flank.
Like a flash they obey the command.
With a terrible yell they attack,
At a gallop they charge on the right,
And they shatter and trample the foe.
The enemy yields all along—
A triumph of right over wrong!

(*Sosia stands immobile, transfixed by his own eloquence.*)

MERCURY

Not a word he's said so far is false, every bit of it is true.

For I was there when the fight was fought, and Father was there too.

SOSIA

The Teleboans took to their heels, and we got added courage.

We fired away at the fleeing foe, and filled their bodies with darts.

And Pterelas, their king, was killed by Amphitryon's own hand.

The fight we fought out there that day went on from dawn to night.

(I remember because, the whole day long, I hadn't had a bite.)

The dark at last separated us, and broke the fighting off.

Next day their leaders, bathed in tears, came from town to us in camp.

They beg, with olive branch outstretched, our pardon for their sins.

They surrender unconditionally: they, each and every one,

Give up to Thebes to treat as it will their city, children, homes.

Amphitryon, for his bravery, was awarded the golden cup

That Pterelas their king once used.

(*Nodding with great satisfaction*)

                                I'll tell all this to his spouse.

(*Abruptly turns and walks toward the door*)

Now to carry out the master's orders. Forward march and into the house!

(*The following speeches are all asides: each speaker, though at times he seems to address the other, actually talks to the audience.*)

MERCURY   Aha! He's heading this way. I'll get going and head him off. I'm not letting him get anywhere near this house today. We look exactly alike, so I'll play a game with him, that's what I'll do. As a matter of fact, since I took his face and figure, it's only right to give myself his character. And that means I have to be canny, tricky, and nasty, and use his own medicine, some nasty trick, to get him away from the door. (*Turning away to look at Sosia*) What's going on? He's looking up at the sky! I'll keep an eye on him and see what he's after.

SOSIA (*staring at the sky, puzzled*)   I swear to god, if there's one thing in this world I'm convinced of beyond any doubt, it's that tonight the Patron God of Night got tight and is sleeping it off. The Big Dipper hasn't budged in the sky, and the moon's in exactly the same place it was when it rose. Orion, Vesper, the Pleiades—none of them has set. All the stars are standing in the same spot; tonight's not moving aside for tomorrow anywhere.

MERCURY (*to the heavens*)   Keep it up, Night. Do what Daddy wants. Do what you might with all your might for the almighty. Best investment you could make.

SOSIA (*as before*)   I don't think I've ever seen a longer night than this. Well, maybe just once, when I got flogged and strung up from dusk till dawn. But, I swear, even that night wasn't as long as this one. If you ask me, the sun's sleeping off a drunk. Did a little overindulging at dinner last night, probably.

MERCURY   Is that so? You stinker, you think gods are like you? Damn you, I'll fix you for such talk—*and* for your bad habits! Just step over here and you'll get what you're not going to like.

SOSIA (*grinning*)   Where are those woman chasers who can't stand going to bed alone? What a chance to give a workout to a high-priced whore who charges by the night!

MERCURY   Judging by what this fellow says, Father's doing the best and smartest thing. He's lying in bed with Alcmena making love, doing what he likes doing most.

SOSIA Well, I'll go in and give Alcmena the report the master ordered me to. (*Starts walking toward the door, catches sight of the figure of Mercury, and comes to an abrupt halt.*) Hey—who's that I see standing in front of the house? At this time of night? I don't like this!

MERCURY (*with a contemptuous gesture in Sosia's direction*) Nobody scares as easily as this one here.

SOSIA (*nervously*) I get it: here I am all dressed up—and he wants to dress me down!

MERCURY (*grinning*) He's scared stiff. I'll have some fun with him.

SOSIA (*as before*) I'm a goner! My jaw has that pre-sock sensation. He's going to greet the homecomer with a kiss from a fist, I know it. He probably feels sorry for me: because my master made me stay awake last night, his knuckles will see to it I get some sleep today. I'm a goner, an absolute goner! I ask you now, look at the size of that bruiser!

MERCURY (*confidentially*) I'll talk out loud in front of him. He'll hear what I say, and get even more scared. (*Loudly*) Come on, fists, it's been ages since you've given me something to slug away in the stomach. That last time—was it only yesterday? Seems like ages ago! You laid four men out. Knocked them stiff.

SOSIA I'm scared he's going to make a change in my family: here I am, an only child, and he's going to make me a quintuplet! He says he knocked out four men; I'm afraid I'm going to raise the figure.

MERCURY (*rolling up his sleeves and taking a boxer's stance, with satisfaction*) There, that's more like it.

SOSIA He's rolling up his sleeves—getting ready for the kill!

MERCURY (*between his teeth*) He's not going to get away from here without a good licking.

SOSIA Who isn't?

MERCURY (*promptly*) Whoever comes this way—he'll eat knuckles!

SOSIA *(hurriedly)* Not me. I don't like eating this late. I already had dinner. Why don't you be smart and serve that dish to people who are hungry?

MERCURY *(caressing one of his fists, with satisfaction)* Real weight in this here fist.

SOSIA Figuring the poundage in his punch! Poor me!

MERCURY *(thoughtfully)* What if I put him to sleep with a soft, slow sock on the jaw?

SOSIA You'll save my life—I haven't been to bed for three nights running.

MERCURY *(throwing a practice haymaker, disgustedly)* Awful! We're not doing well at all. These knuckles just won't learn how to sock a jaw. One tap with this fist, and I should be able to change a man's looks.

SOSIA He's like the fellows who fix up statues! He's going to make me a new face!

MERCURY *(to his fist)* If you really hit a man, you should knock every bone out of his head.

SOSIA Say, maybe he's thinking of filleting my face like a fish! Keep me from a fellow who fillets folks! If he catches sight of me, I'm done for!

MERCURY *(elaborately sniffing the air)* I smell someone—and he'll be sorry!

SOSIA Oh, my god, did he get a whiff of me?

MERCURY *(with more intensive sniffing)* He was far away before, but he can't be very far now.

SOSIA *(flabbergasted)* This guy's a magician!

MERCURY *(throwing a series of fast jabs)* These fists are bucking like a bronco.

SOSIA If you're going to give them a workout on me, please break them in on the wall first!

MERCURY *(suddenly stops his shadow boxing and stands still, cocking an ear; burlesquing the style of grand opera)* Somebody's words have winged their way to mine ears!

SOSIA What rotten luck! Why didn't I clip its wings? *I* have to have a voice like a bird!

MERCURY (*snarling*) He's going to get it from me. I'll fix his wagon.

SOSIA (*promptly*) I haven't got a wagon.

MERCURY (*as before*) I'll give him a load of fist.

SOSIA (*resentfully*) I'm all worn out from the trip back on the boat, I'm still seasick, I can barely walk *without* carrying anything, so don't get the idea I can take any loads.

MERCURY No question about it—I hear somebody talking.

SOSIA Saved! He doesn't see me. He says Somebody's talking. One thing I know: my name's Sosia, not Somebody.

MERCURY (*turning toward Sosia, burlesquing the style of grand opera*) Here from the right, methinks a voice strikes mine ears.

SOSIA (*despondently*) My voice struck him, eh? I'm afraid *I'll* get struck to even the score. (*Takes a tentative step away.*)

MERCURY (*ironically*) He's coming my way. Perfect.

SOSIA (*stopping dead in his tracks*) I'm so scared, I'm numb all over! I swear, I couldn't tell you where in the world I am right now, if you asked me. I'm so scared I can't even move! This is it: this is the end of the master's orders—and Sosia along with them. (*Eyes Mercury uncertainly, notices that he is not moving, and screws up his courage.*) All right. My mind's made up: I'll talk back to him. That way I'll look like someone with guts, and he'll keep his hands off me.

(*Sosia, swinging his lantern jauntily, swaggers up to the door. The two now address each other instead of the audience.*)

MERCURY (*in his grand opera style*) Whither away, O stranger with Vulcan's fire in that piece of horn?

SOSIA (*belligerently*) What do you want to know for, O stranger who fillets faces with his fists?

MERCURY (*menacingly*)   Are you a slave or not?

SOSIA (*shrugging*)   Whichever I like.

MERCURY (*arms akimbo, jaw out*)   Is that so?

SOSIA (*arms akimbo, jaw out*)   Yeah, that's so.

MERCURY (*contemptuously*)   You deserve a good licking.

SOSIA   That's a lie!

MERCURY (*rolling up his sleeves and making other ominous preparations*)   You're going to tell me it's the truth. I'll see to that right now.

SOSIA (*his courage rapidly becoming unscrewed*)   Now, why do you have to do that?

MERCURY (*ominously*)   I want to know where you're going, who you belong to, and what you came for. How about it?

SOSIA (*blandly*)   I came here, and I'm my master's servant. Any the wiser now?

MERCURY (*as before*)   Damn you, I'll stop that mouth of yours!

SOSIA (*girlishly fluttering his eyes, and demurely putting his hands over his lips*)   Oh sir, you can't! It's a very proper mouth, and I take good care of it.

MERCURY (*grimly*)   More nonsense out of you? What are you doing around this house?

SOSIA   What are *you* doing here?

MERCURY   Orders from King Creon. One man stands guard all night every night.

SOSIA (*grandly*)   Very nice of him. Takes good care of the house because he knows we're away. (*Taking a step forward and airily waving Mercury aside*) You can leave now. Tell him the family's back.

MERCURY (*blocking the way*)   I don't know how you can belong to this family. And, "family man," unless you take off this minute, you're not going to get treated like one of the family!

SOSIA (*stubbornly*)   I tell you I live here. I'm a servant here.

MERCURY Do you know what's going to happen to you? If you don't get out of here, I'm going to make you into a real aristocrat.

SOSIA How's that?

MERCURY Once I get my hands on a club, you won't walk away from here, you'll be carried.

SOSIA (*desperately*) But I tell you I'm one of the family! A family servant.

MERCURY You're not leaving this minute? Then kindly figure out how soon you want your licking.

SOSIA You think you're going to keep me out of this house after I came all the way here from overseas?

MERCURY (*incredulously*) This is your house?

SOSIA Of course.

MERCURY Then who's your master?

SOSIA Amphitryon. He's off now commanding the Theban army. Alcmena's his wife.

MERCURY Tell me, what's your name?

SOSIA (*drawing himself up; in the <u>grand opera style</u>*) Men call me Sosia. Sprung from the loins of Davus am I.[2]

MERCURY (*eying him distastefully*) You've got a nerve! You'll pay for this. Coming here this way with a pack of lies, and dirty schemes on foot!

SOSIA (*reproachfully*) I came here with my shoes on foot, not dirty schemes.

MERCURY (*promptly*) Still lying—you came here with your feet on shoes. (*Roars at his joke.*)

SOSIA (*deciding it would be politic to acknowledge this sally, roaring too*) You're absolutely right.

MERCURY (*suddenly switching off the laughter*) Then you're absolutely going to get a beating for telling lies.

SOSIA But I absolutely don't want one.

---

[2] "Men call me Joe. Sprung from the loins of Mike, etc." will give some idea of the joke.

MERCURY   But you're absolutely going to get one, whether you want it or not. When I say "absolutely," my mind's made up; there's no room for discussion. (*Starts clobbering Sosia.*)

SOSIA   Don't! Please! I beg you!

MERCURY   (*continuing the clobbering*)   Where do you get the nerve to say you're Sosia when I'm Sosia?

SOSIA   He's murdering me!

MERCURY   Murder isn't anything compared with what's coming. Who's your master?

SOSIA   (*hurriedly*)   You are. Those fists of yours have given you right of possession. (*At the top of his lungs*) Men of Thebes! Help!

MERCURY   (*silencing him with a punch*)   So you'll yell, will you, you stinker! Now speak up! What did you come here for?

SOSIA   (*bitterly*)   So you could have somebody to beat to a pulp.

MERCURY   Who's your master?

SOSIA   (*doggedly*)   Amphitryon. I'm his servant Sosia.

MERCURY   That means you're going to get beaten up even more for talking nonsense. *I'm* Sosia, not you.

SOSIA   (*muttering to himself*)   God, do I wish it! You be me, and then I'll beat *you* up.

MERCURY   (*snarling*)   What are you muttering about?

SOSIA   (*hurriedly*)   I'll keep quiet.

MERCURY   Who's your master?

SOSIA   Whoever you say.

MERCURY   Now tell me this: what's your name?

SOSIA   Whatever name you say.

MERCURY   (*glowering*)   You told me you were Amphitryon's Sosia.

SOSIA   I made a mistake. I meant to say I was Amphitryon's *associate*.

MERCURY (*nodding satisfiedly*)   I knew darn well the family
had only one Sosia—me. You dropped the ball there.

SOSIA (*aside*)   I wish to god you'd do that with those fists!

MERCURY (*emphatically*)   I'm the Sosia you were trying to
tell me a minute ago you were.

SOSIA (*in desperation*)   Will you do me a favor? Will you
please let me talk to you in peace, without getting beaten
up?

MERCURY   No peace—just a temporary truce, if there's something you want to say.

SOSIA (*quickly*)   I don't talk without a treaty of peace—
you're stronger than I am, you can lick me.

MERCURY (*with an air of magnanimity*)   Say what you
want. I won't hurt you.

SOSIA   You give me your word?

MERCURY   Word of honor.

SOSIA (*suspiciously*)   What if you go back on it?

MERCURY (*in his grand opera style*)   Then may the wrath of
Mercury fall upon Sosia!

SOSIA (*suddenly regaining his aplomb*)   Well, now that I
can say what I want to, you listen here: *I'm* Amphitryon's
servant Sosia.

MERCURY (*advancing on him menacingly*)   What, again?

SOSIA (*doggedly*)   We made peace, we signed a treaty, so
I'm telling you the truth.

MERCURY   I'm going to beat you up!

SOSIA (*as before*)   You can do whatever you like with me,
because you're stronger than I am, you can lick me. (*At
the top of his lungs*) But, no matter what you do to me,
this is one thing, damn it all, I'm not going to keep quiet
about!

MERCURY (*grimly*)   You're not going to stop me from being
Sosia, not as long as you live.

SOSIA   And, damn it all, you're not going to make me be

somebody different from myself. I'm the only servant Sosia
we've got in the family. I'm the fellow who went off with
Amphitryon to the front.

MERCURY (*to the world at large*)   This fellow's out of his
mind!

SOSIA   That's what's wrong with you, not me! (*To himself*)
What the devil! Ain't I Amphitryon's servant Sosia? Didn't
our ship arrive just tonight from the port of the Teleboans
with me aboard? Didn't my own master send me here?
Ain't I standing in front of my own house right this min-
ute? Don't I have a lantern in my hand? Ain't I talking?
Ain't I awake? Didn't this fellow here just now beat me up?
(*Groaning*) He sure did! My jaw still aches. (*Resolutely*)
What am I waiting for? Why don't I go right into my
house?

MERCURY   What do you mean, *your* house?

SOSIA (*doggedly*)   That's what I said.

MERCURY   Oh no. Every word you just said is a lie. *I'm*
Amphitryon's Sosia. Tonight our ship cleared the land of
the Teleboans with *me* on board. It was after we stormed
and took King Pterelas' town and beat the Teleboan army
by some hard fighting, and Amphitryon killed King Pterelas
with his own hands during the battle.

SOSIA (*to the audience, flabbergasted*)   Even I don't believe
I'm me when I hear him say these things! No doubt about
it—this fellow's got everything that happened there down
pat! (*To Mercury*) Tell me this: what was Amphitryon
presented with out of the booty from the Teleboans?

MERCURY (*promptly*)   The gold cup King Pterelas used to
drink out of.

SOSIA (*to the audience, glumly*)   That's the right answer.
(*To Mercury*) Where's the cup now?

MERCURY (*as before*)   In a chest. Locked and sealed with
Amphitryon's seal.

SOSIA   What is his seal?

MERCURY   The rising sun in a four-horse chariot. (*Snarling*) You trying to catch me, damn you?

SOSIA (*to the audience, in despair*)   He's convinced me. I'll have to find another name! I don't know where he could have seen all this. (*Stands glumly for a moment, then is electrified by an idea.*) Wait! Now I'll get him. After all, what I did all by myself in the tent, with no one else around, that's something he'll never be able to tell me, *never*. (*To Mercury, brimming with confidence*) Well, if you're Sosia, what were you busy doing in the tent when the fighting was going on fast and furious? You tell me that, and I give up.

MERCURY (*slowly and with great precision*)   There was a keg of wine. I filled a jug from it.

SOSIA (*to the audience, nervously*)   He's on the right track.

MERCURY   Then I put away the whole jugful, neat, just the way it came from mother grape.

SOSIA (*to the audience, dumb struck*)   That's just what happened! I put away a jugful of wine, neat. (*Savagely*) I'll bet he was hiding there inside that jug.

MERCURY   Well? Have I convinced you you're not Sosia?

SOSIA (*belligerently*)   You're telling me I'm not, eh?

MERCURY (*shrugging*)   What else can I tell you, when *I* am?

SOSIA (*with hand over heart*)   I swear by Jove that *I* am, and I swear that's no lie.

MERCURY (*with hand over heart*)   And I swear by Mercury that Jove doesn't believe you. Take my word, he'll sooner believe me without an oath than you with.

SOSIA (*desperately*)   Well then, who am I, if I'm not Sosia? Answer me that!

MERCURY   When I'm done being Sosia, you go right ahead and be Sosia. But right now *I'm* Sosia, so either you beat it or get a beating, Anonymous!

(*Sosia goes up to him, looks him over, and then steps back scratching his head.*)

SOSIA (*to the audience, baffled*) So help me, when I look at him I recognize all my features, there's no doubt about it! I've seen myself in the mirror lots of times, and he's exactly like me. He's got the same hat and clothes. (*Peering harder*) He's my spitting image! Legs, feet, height, haircut, eyes, nose, lips, jaws, chin, beard, neck, everything. What else is there to say? If he's got whip-scars all over his back, no two items in this world could be more alike. (*Clutching his head*) Yet, when I think it over, I'm the same person I've always been, no question about it! I know my master's name, I know our house, I can use my head, and I've got all my senses. (*Plucking up courage*) I won't pay any attention to what he says; I'll knock on the door. (*Starts walking up to the door.*)

MERCURY (*blocking the way*) Where do you think you're going?

SOSIA Home.

MERCURY (*grimly*) You could climb aboard Jove's own magic chariot this minute to try to get away, but it wouldn't do you a bit of good: you're in for trouble and you're going to get it!

SOSIA (*weakly*) Can't I give my mistress the report my master ordered me to?

MERCURY You can give *your* mistress whatever you want. But I'm not letting you get anywhere near mine. (*Thundering*) Now, don't get me sore or you'll be carried out of here with those legs of yours stove in!

SOSIA (*with alacrity*) Oh no! I'm going. (*Raising his eyes to heaven*) God in heaven, please! Where did I lose myself? Where did I get changed over? Where did I drop my looks? Did I forget myself and leave myself at the pier? Because this fellow here's got hold of the exact same looks I used to have. He's my statue—something nobody'll ever give me when I'm dead, I've already got while alive! (*Eyes Mercury standing resolutely in front of the door and shrugs helplessly.*) I'll go back to the pier and tell the master every-

thing that's happened. (*Mournfully*) Maybe he won't recognize me either. (*Brightening*) I hope to god he doesn't!
I'll have these slave clothes off me and a free man's on, in
no time! (*Dashes off, stage right.*)

MERCURY (*to the audience, with great satisfaction*)   This
job went off very nicely. *Very* nicely. I got that blamed
nuisance away from the door, and (*gesturing toward the
house*) Father can stay on in her arms in peace. (*Grinning*)
When that fellow gets back there to his master, he'll tell
Amphitryon that Sosia the servant drove him away from
the door. Amphitryon'll think he's lying and that he dis-
obeyed orders and never even came here. (*Gleefully*) I'll
get both of them all mixed up and drive them and Amphitryon's whole household crazy, until Father's had enough
of his inamorata. Then, when it's all over, they'll all find
out what happened, and Jove at the end will restore Alcmena and her husband to their former married bliss. You
see, Amphitryon is going to raise an awful ruckus with his
wife and accuse her of adultery, but Father will step in
and put down the insurrection.

(*Starts to go toward the door, then suddenly stops,
struck by a new idea.*) There's something I didn't mention
before about Alcmena. She's going to give birth today to
twins, two boys. One will be a full-term baby, the other
just a six-month baby. One is Amphitryon's, the other
Jove's; the littler baby has the greater father, and vice
versa. You all sure you understand the situation?

(*Looks the faces over anxiously and, reassured, continues.*) For the sake of Alcmena's reputation, Father's fixed
it so there'll be only one confinement: she'll be done with
two birth pangs in one labor. That way no one'll suspect
anything illicit, and this clandestine cohabiting will stay a
secret. However, as I mentioned before, Amphitryon will
be told the whole story. What's the difference? Alcmena's
reputation won't be hurt the least little bit. After all, it
wouldn't do for a god to let *his* sin and guilt fall on the
head of a mortal. (*His attention caught, looks toward the*

door.) I'll shut up now—there's a sound at the door. Here comes the fake Amphitryon with Alcmena, the wife he has on loan.

(*The door opens and Jove and Alcmena step out.*

Alcmena, a ravishingly beautiful woman, perhaps in her early thirties, has more than mere good looks: her face shines with a candor and purity that add a special radiance to her loveliness.

Her consort is a strongly built, handsome man in his forties. By the way he carries himself you can sense immediately that he is used to giving, not taking orders. He carries a stick, and is dressed in traveling clothes topped off by a broad-brimmed hat that has a tiny gold tassel dangling down behind.)

JOVE (*holding both her hands, tenderly*) Good-by, Alcmena dear. Take good care of our household, as you're doing. And please take things easy! You can see for yourself that your time is very near now. I've got to run along. (*Gravely*) Whether it's a girl or a boy—I want the child to be brought up.

ALCMENA (*plaintively*) What's come up, dear, to make you leave home so suddenly?

JOVE (*tenderly*) Believe me, it's not because I'm tired either of you or of being home. But, when the commander in chief isn't with his troops, things that don't need doing get done with lots more dispatch than things that do.

MERCURY (*to the audience, gesturing toward Jove*) A smooth operator, this one here. (*Grinning*) And why not? He's *my* father.[3] Watch how he's going to butter the girl up.

ALCMENA (*pouting*) Well! I can certainly see how much *you* care for your wife.

JOVE (*kissing her*) Isn't it enough for you that I love you more than any other woman in the world?

MERCURY (*aside, gesturing toward the sky where presumably*

---

[3] Mercury was patron god of thieves.

Juno is)   If that one up there finds out that you're busy with things like this, believe me, you'll wish you were Amphitryon instead of Jove!

ALCMENA (*as before*)   I'd rather find out for myself than be told. Before your place in bed has had time to get warm, you're on your way! You arrived just yesterday in the middle of the night, and now you're leaving. Do you think I like this?

MERCURY (*to the audience*)   I'll go up and have a word with her. Play Helpful Henry for Pappa. (*Walking up to Alcmena and addressing her*) So help me, I don't think there's a man on earth who's as mad about his wife as he's mad about you. (*Glances covertly to observe the effect of this on Jove.*)

JOVE (*to Mercury, thundering*)   God damn you! Think I don't know what you're up to! Out of my sight! What do you think you're doing, messing into my affairs? What do you think you're doing, opening that big mouth of yours? (*Brandishing his stick*) Why, I'll take this stick and I'll—

ALCMENA (*interrupting in alarm*)   Don't, please!

JOVE (*snarling*)   Just let him open that big mouth of his!

MERCURY (*to the audience, grinning*)   My debut as Helpful Henry was almost a fiasco.

JOVE (*conciliatorily*)   But to get back to what you were saying, dear. You really shouldn't be angry with me. I sneaked away from headquarters. I stole this chance to see you, so I could be the first to tell you, and you the first to hear, how I served my country. And now you've heard all about it. Would I do such a thing if I didn't love you very, very much?

MERCURY (*to the audience, chuckling*)   Didn't I tell you he'd do this? A little buttering up, and he has the poor girl eating out of his hand.

JOVE   And now I've got to sneak back, so the men won't find out and say I think more of my wife than my country.

ALCMENA (*starting to cry*) You have your poor wife in tears by going away like this.

JOVE (*tenderly*) Sh! Don't spoil those pretty eyes. I'll be back very soon.

ALCMENA (*sobbing*) That "very soon" is such a long, long time!

JOVE (*as before*) Believe me, I'm not very happy about going away and leaving you.

ALCMENA (*bitterly*) Oh sure—that's why you're leaving the same night you came. (*She reaches out to hold him by the arm.*)

JOVE (*gently taking her hand away*) You mustn't hold me back. It's getting late. I want to be out of the city before dawn. (*He holds up a box.*) Here's the cup which was awarded to me for gallantry in action. King Pterelas used to own it; I killed him with my own hands. (*Handing it to her*) It's a present for you, Alcmena.

ALCMENA (*smiling radiantly through her tears*) You're always doing things like that! It's a wonderful gift, as wonderful as the giver.

MERCURY (*bowing gallantly*) Say rather a wonderful gift, as wonderful as the *getter*.

JOVE (*turning on him*) Still at it? Damn you, can't I get rid of you!

ALCMENA (*stroking his cheek*) Please Amphitryon, don't be angry at Sosia. For my sake.

JOVE (*grumbling*) Well, anything to please you.

MERCURY (*to the audience, gesturing toward Jove*) What love does to him! So touchy!

JOVE (*kissing her good-by*) Anything you want before I go?

ALCMENA Yes. Love me even though I'm far away—since I'm all yours, even though you're far away.

MERCURY (*impatiently*) Let's go, Amphitryon! It's already getting light.

JOVE   You go ahead, Sosia. I'll be along in a minute. (*Mercury leaves, stage left. Jove kisses Alcmena again.*) Nothing I can do for you?

ALCMENA   Yes—come back soon. (*She waves a last good-by, then swiftly turns and runs into the house.*)

JOVE (*calling after her*)   All right. (*Winking at the audience*) I'll be back sooner than you think! So cheer up.

(*He turns and, raising his head, addresses the sky.*)

Night, you waited very patiently. You're dismissed; make way for Day. Let Day now spread its clear bright light over the earth. And, Night, to even things up I'll make the day shorter by exactly as much time as you were longer than the night before. Go now—let the dark give way to light!

(*To the audience*)

And now I'll go and follow Mercury.

(*He exits, stage left, and the stage is now empty.*)

ACT II

(It is now some hours later, and day has dawned. Enter, stage right, Amphitryon, then Sosia, then some porters carrying baggage. Amphitryon is identical in appearance with the Jove of the last act, save for the telltale tassel.)

SONG

AMPHITRYON *(impatiently)*
>Come on! Shake a leg and follow me!

SOSIA *(hurrying to keep up)*
>I am, I'm right behind you, see?

AMPHITRYON *(stopping and eying him distastefully)*
>You're a worthless good-for-nothing, I'd say.

SOSIA *(innocently)*
>But why? What makes you feel that way?

AMPHITRYON *(angrily)*
>Because you stand there telling me
>What never was and never will be.

SOSIA *(shaking his head despondently)*
>You see? You're always doing it.
>You won't trust any of us one bit.

AMPHITRYON *(working himself up)*
>Now what do you mean by that! I swear,
>You good-for-nothing, I'm going to tear
>That good-for-nothing tongue of yours out!

SOSIA *(doggedly)*
>I belong to you, so I've no doubt
>You'll do to me what it suits you to.
>But nothing you can possibly do
>Will make me say this isn't true.

AMPHITRYON *(exploding)*
>You're standing here and yet, you louse,
>You've the nerve to tell me you're now in the
>>house!

SOSIA (*as before*)
>   That's true.

AMPHITRYON
>   Well, god will punish you—
>   And, damn it all, *I* will too.

SOSIA (*sulkily*)
>   You're master here. All I do is serve.

AMPHITRYON (*in a towering rage*)
>   I want to know where you get the nerve
>   To play your jokes on me,
>   To tell me a thing no man has seen,
>   A thing which just can't be.
>   Of all the barefaced impudence!
>   Of all the brazen stunts!
>   To tell me that the selfsame man
>   Can be in two places at once!

SOSIA (*as before*)
>   I tell you that's what happened to me.

AMPHITRYON
>   Oh, you be damned!

SOSIA (*reproachfully*)
>   But I don't see
>   What I've done to earn these threats from you.

AMPHITRYON
>   You dare to ask, you stinker, you,
>   When you stand there laughing in my face?

SOSIA (*doggedly*)
>   If what I'd said was not the case,
>   Then I'd deserve these damns from you.
>   But it's not a lie. Every word is true,
>   I'm giving you the story straight.

AMPHITRYON (*looking at him in disgust*)
>   The fellow's drunk, as sure as fate.

SOSIA (*despairingly*)
>   I wish I were!

AMPHITRYON (*acidly*)

You wish to do
What's already done?

SOSIA (*bewildered*)

Who me?

AMPHITRYON (*icily*)

Yes you.
Just where did you find the liquor, pray?

SOSIA

Me? Nowhere. Haven't touched a drop today.

AMPHITRYON (*to the world at large, throwing up his hands
   helplessly*)

What kind of man is this, anyway!

SOSIA (*expostulating, pointing to the house*)

By now I've said it ten times, I swear.
   Must I holler in your ear?
I tell you I'm in that house over there,
   And also beside you here.
You think that now the situation
   Is sufficiently plain and clear?

AMPHITRYON (*shouting*)

Stand back from me! Why, this is outrageous!

SOSIA

Why, what's the matter now?

AMPHITRYON (*witheringly*)

You're contagious—
You've caught the plague.

SOSIA (*reproachfully*)

Why say such a thing?
I'm in the pink, my health's just flourishing!

AMPHITRYON (*snarling*)

I'll bet it doesn't stay that way!
You'll get what's coming to you today:
If I make it home, I guarantee
You'll live a life of misery!

(*He glares at Sosia balefully in silence for a moment, and then resumes.*)

(*Icily*)   Follow me, faithful servant who makes a fool of his master by talking drivel, who, on top of neglecting to carry out his master's orders, deliberately comes to laugh in his master's face, who hands his master an impossible story, something no one's ever heard of even through hearsay—AND whose back, believe you me, will pay for every last one of his lies.

SOSIA (*reproachfully*)   Amphitryon, I can't tell you how unhappy it makes an honest servant, one who tells his master the honest truth, to see the truth take a beating.

AMPHITRYON (*as before*)   Then let's you and I figure it out: how the devil is it possible for you, at this very moment, to be right here and also in the house? That's what I want to know.

SOSIA   It's absolutely true: I'm here and I'm there. If this sounds like a miracle, it's just as much a miracle to me as it is to you.

AMPHITRYON   How's that?

SOSIA (*grinning*)   Since it's no less a miracle to me than to you. (*Becoming serious again*) So help me, at first I didn't believe in my other me, until my other me convinced me to believe in him. He reeled off the whole story, down to the last detail, of what happened at the front. And he stole my looks along with my name: two drops of milk aren't as alike as my other me is to me. (*Thoughtfully*) You see, when you sent me home from the pier before daybreak a little while ago—

AMPHITRYON (*interrupting impatiently*)   Well, what about it?

SOSIA (*ignoring the interruption*)   —I'd already been standing in front of the house long before I arrived there.

AMPHITRYON (*throwing up his hands*)   What the devil is this nonsense! Are you in your right mind?

SOSIA (*glumly*)   See for yourself.

AMPHITRYON (*tapping his temple significantly; to himself, portentously*)   After he left me, he must have seen the evil eye. Had some evil strike him.

SOSIA (*promptly*)   I sure did: I got beaten to a pulp.

AMPHITRYON   Who beat you?

SOSIA (*as before*)   I did myself. (*As Amphitryon looks at him bewildered*) The me who's in the house now.

AMPHITRYON (*with deadly calm*)   Now watch out. I want only answers to my questions, nothing more. First of all— this other Sosia of yours, who is he? That's what I want to know.

SOSIA   Your servant.

AMPHITRYON (*groaning*)   Even one of you is more than I want! (*Pounding his fist into the palm of his hand*) I've owned only one Sosia in all my life, and that's you!

SOSIA (*shaking his head stubbornly*)   I'll tell you right here and now, Amphitryon: I bet you, when you get home, you'll run into another servant Sosia in addition to me in the house. His father's name was Davus just like mine, he looks exactly like me, and he's the same age. To put it in a nutshell, your Sosia's become twins.

AMPHITRYON (*baffled*)   This is a very strange story. (*After a moment's thought*) Did you get to see my wife?

SOSIA   How? I wasn't allowed into the house.

AMPHITRYON   Who stopped you?

SOSIA   The other Sosia I've been telling you about, the one who beat me up.

AMPHITRYON (*thundering*)   Who is that Sosia?

SOSIA   Me, I tell you! How many times must I say it?

AMPHITRYON (*suddenly struck by a thought, eying him suspiciously*)   Say, tell me this—you weren't asleep a little while ago, were you?

SOSIA (*shaking his head vigorously*)   Not the least little bit.

AMPHITRYON   I was wondering whether maybe you had seen some Sosia in a dream.

SOSIA (*in high dudgeon*)   I am not in the habit of carrying out my master's orders in a comatose condition. I was wide awake when I saw him, I'm wide awake now seeing you, I'm wide awake now telling you this story, and I was wide awake a little while ago when I got beaten up. He was wide awake too.

AMPHITRYON   Who was?

SOSIA (*wearily*)   The other Sosia, I tell you. (*Pleadingly*) Please! Can't you understand?

AMPHITRYON (*helplessly*)   How the devil could anyone understand! You talk such drivel!

SOSIA (*grimly*)   You'll understand soon enough, when you see that Sosia standing in front of your eyes.

AMPHITRYON (*starting off toward the door, grimly*)   Then follow me. The first thing I've got to do is look into this whole business.

(*He strides up to the door and looks it over. Then, with Sosia and the porters at his heels, he moves away to examine the rest of the house from the outside. As they do so, the door opens and, unnoticed by them, Alcmena steps out.*)

SONG

ALCMENA (*to the audience, sadly*)
> As we go through life, how rare is happiness
> Compared with misery! It's part of life
> For everyone, it's heaven's pleasure that
> Sorrow travel hand in hand with joy,
> That, once some good has happened, on its heels
> There follow even more of toil and trouble.
> You see, just now I learned this for myself,
> I know it from my own experience.
> I was given a moment of joy, the chance I had
> To see my husband. It lasted just a night;
> Before the day had come, he suddenly

Arose and went away. And now I feel
I'm utterly alone, since he whom I
Love best of all no longer is with me.
His leaving brought me more of sorrow than
His coming brought me joy.

(*Pauses, and then, her countenance brightening, resumes proudly*)

Yet one thing's made me happy: he conquered his foes
And came back home bearing a crown of glory.
This is my consolation; he may always leave
My side if it is to return to me a hero.
The parting will hurt, but I will bear the hurt
With strength and resolution if this one
Reward I get: to see my husband hailed
By all as victor on the field of battle.
For me just this is enough. Our greatest prize
Is courage—courage takes, beyond all doubt,
First place among all things upon this earth.
Our lives, our liberty, safety, all we own,
Our parents, children, homes, and fatherland—
Courage is the guardian of them all.
For courage embraces every good there is;
If a man has courage, every good is his!

(*She falls silent. A moment later, Amphitryon and his entourage return from their inspection of the house. Alcmena, unnoticed, remains buried in thought near the door.*)

AMPHITRYON (*to Sosia, enthusiastically*) I know my wife will be overjoyed to see me back. (*Smiling happily, half to himself*) We're very much in love with each other. (*To Sosia*) Especially since everything's gone so well—I led the army to victory, I defeated at the first encounter an enemy everyone thought invincible. Yes, I'm sure of it; she simply can't wait to see me back.

SOSIA What about me? You think that lady friend of mine won't be glad to see *me?*

ALCMENA (*her attention caught by the sound of voices, in surprise*)   There's my husband!

AMPHITRYON (*to Sosia, heading for the door*)   Follow me.

ALCMENA (*to herself*)   What's he coming back for? A little while ago he was saying he was in a hurry to get away. (*Puzzled*) Is he deliberately trying to test me? Does he want to see for himself how I miss him when he's away? (*Smiling happily*) Well, I certainly have no objections to having him back!

SOSIA (*suddenly catching sight of Alcmena and stopping in his tracks*)   Amphitryon, we'd better go back to the ship.

AMPHITRYON (*also stopping; puzzled*)   Why?

SOSIA   Because no one's going to give us homecomers breakfast.

AMPHITRYON (*as before*)   Now what put that idea in your head?

SOSIA   We're too late.

AMPHITRYON   How's that?

SOSIA   There's Alcmena in front of the door. And I can see she's got a full belly.

AMPHITRYON (*looking and smiling*)   Oh, she was pregnant when I left.

SOSIA (*groaning*)   My god! That's the end of me!

AMPHITRYON   What's the matter?

SOSIA   If I follow your figuring, she must be in her ninth month. That means I've come home just in time to start hauling water!

AMPHITRYON (*smiling*)   Come on, cheer up.

SOSIA   Cheer up? Oh, sure! (*Savagely*) Just let me get my hands on a bucket. God damn it, never believe a word I say from this minute on if I don't draw the last drop of life out of that damn well once I get started!

AMPHITRYON   Come along. Don't worry; I'll give someone else the job.

ALCMENA (*to herself, excitedly*)   I think I really should run up to meet him.

(*She walks swiftly up to him, holding out her hands. He takes them in his and looks at her, smiling blissfully.*)

AMPHITRYON (*warmly*)   Joyful greetings from Amphitryon to his darling wife—the finest wife in all Thebes, in her husband's considered opinion, and a good woman too, as every husband in Thebes will tell you. (*Drawing her closer, tenderly*) How have you been, dear? Are you glad to see me?

(*There is a moment of silence as Alcmena stares at him uncomprehendingly.*)

SOSIA (*aside, acidly*)   Never saw anybody more glad. Giving him about as warm a greeting as you would a stray mutt!

AMPHITRYON (*as before*)   And to see you pregnant this way and so near your time! I'm simply delighted!

ALCMENA (*bewildered*)   Will you please tell me why you must make fun of me like this with these salutations and greetings? As if you didn't see me just a little while ago! As if you've just this minute come back from the front! (*Curiously*) Why this greeting me as if you hadn't seen me for ages?

AMPHITRYON (*taken aback*)   Why, I haven't laid eyes on you until just now!

ALCMENA (*as before*)   Now what makes you say that?

AMPHITRYON (*as before*)   Because I've learned to tell the truth!

ALCMENA (*annoyed*)   Well, a man who unlearns what he's learned is not behaving well at all! Are you two trying to test my feelings? (*Softening her tone as she notices their genuine bewilderment*) What brings you back so quickly? A bad omen hold you back? The weather keeping you from sailing to the front, as you said you were going to do a little while ago?

AMPHITRYON   "A little while ago?" How little a while ago
was this little while ago?

ALCMENA (*resentfully*)   You're trying to catch me! (*With a
careless wave of the hand, irritably*) Some time ago. Just
before.

AMPHITRYON (*throwing up his hands*)   Now will you kindly
explain how that's possible? (*Mimicking her*) "Some time
ago. Just before."

ALCMENA (*acidly*)   What do you think? That, because
you're making fun of me, I'm making fun of you? Imagine
telling me that this is the first I've seen of you when you
just left here a little while ago!

AMPHITRYON (*to Sosia, incredulously*)   She's talking raving
nonsense!

SOSIA (*to Amphitryon, with an I-understand-the-whole-busi-
ness air*)   Just wait a little while, until she sleeps off this
dream.

AMPHITRYON   You mean she dreams while she's wide awake?

ALCMENA (*to Amphitryon, sharply*)   I most certainly am
wide awake, and I'm telling you what happened with these
eyes of mine wide open. A little while ago, just before daybreak, I saw both you and (*gesturing contemptuously toward Sosia*) him.

AMPHITRYON   Where?

ALCMENA   Here, in your own house.

AMPHITRYON (*brusquely*)   You never did!

SOSIA (*to Amphitryon*)   Wait a second. (*Eagerly*) What if
the ship brought us from the dock to the door here in our
sleep?

AMPHITRYON (*witheringly*)   Are you on her side too?

SOSIA (*whispering urgently*)   What do you expect? Don't
you understand? If you try to say no to a madwoman,
you'll make the crazy thing crazier, and she'll keep clobbering you. Say yes to her, and she'll let you off with only
one sock.

AMPHITRYON (*to Sosia, grimly*)   There's one thing that's going to happen right now: I'm going to give her a piece of my mind for not giving me a greeting on my return home.

SOSIA (*to Amphitryon*)   You'll stir up a hornet's nest!

AMPHITRYON (*to Sosia*)   Quiet! (*To Alcmena*) Alcmena, I want to ask you something.

ALCMENA (*shrugging*)   Go ahead. Anything you like.

AMPHITRYON (*angrily*)   Have you had an attack of stupidity? Or an overdose of the feeling that no one's good enough for you?

ALCMENA (*helplessly*)   My dear husband, whatever put the idea in your head to ask me a question like that?

AMPHITRYON (*bitterly*)   Because, up to now, you always used to come up and greet me the way any decent, loving wife would greet a husband. Now I come home and find you completely changed!

ALCMENA (*earnestly*)   But I did! My dear, the very moment you arrived yesterday, I greeted you. I asked how you were, I took your hand, and I kissed you.

SOSIA (*to Alcmena, uncomprehendingly*)   You greeted him yesterday?

ALCMENA   You too, Sosia.

SOSIA (*to Amphitryon, shaking his head mournfully*)   Amphitryon, I had hoped she would bear you a son, but she's not big with child.

AMPHITRYON   With what, then?

SOSIA   With bats in her belfry!

ALCMENA (*to Sosia, acidly*)   I am perfectly sound, and god willing, I'll be safe when I give birth. (*Gesturing toward Amphitryon*) And if he'd only do his duty, you'd get a good smack of the whip! (*Raising her voice*) You'd get what you deserve for putting a jinx like that on me, you jinxer you!

SOSIA (*muttering to himself, sullenly*)   Yeah? A pregnant woman should get a good smack—(*catching Alcmena's*

glare and switching abruptly to bright innocence) a snack,
I mean. You know, something to nibble on in case she
starts to feel nauseous.

AMPHITRYON (to Alcmena)   You saw me here yesterday?

ALCMENA (wearily)   If you must be told for the tenth time,
yes!

AMPHITRYON (hopefully)   In a dream, maybe?

ALCMENA (as before)   No. I was wide awake, and so were
you.

AMPHITRYON (to the world at large)   The troubles I have!

SOSIA   What's the matter?

AMPHITRYON   My wife's gone crazy!

SOSIA (gloomily, nodding knowledgeably)   Sudden attack of
manic depression. Nothing like it for driving people mad.

AMPHITRYON (solicitously)   When did you first feel this
coming on, Alcmena?

ALCMENA (preserving an icy calm)   I tell you, I am not
crazy.

AMPHITRYON   Then why do you say you saw me yesterday,
when I only arrived in port last night? I had dinner there,
and I slept all night on board. (Emphatically) I haven't
put foot inside this house since the day I left with the army
to fight the Teleboans. And, what's more, defeated them.

ALCMENA (as before)   That's not so. You had dinner with
me, and you slept with me.

AMPHITRYON (roaring)   What did you say?

ALCMENA (as before)   The truth.

AMPHITRYON (grimly)   Not about that, it isn't. About anything else, I wouldn't know.

ALCMENA (as before)   And, at the crack of dawn, you left
for the front.

AMPHITRYON (frantically)   How can this be?

SOSIA (promptly)   She's telling it just as she remembers it.
It's a dream she's telling you. (To Alcmena, shaking his

head regretfully) But, after you woke up, Alcmena, you should have offered special prayers to Jove. He's our patron god of miracles, you know.

ALCMENA (*disgusted*)   Oh, go to the devil!

SOSIA (*muttering to himself*)   No, you go—(*catching her glare and switching abruptly to bright innocence*) and take care of those prayers. Do you good.

ALCMENA (*to Amphitryon, grimly*)   That's the second time he's insulted me, and you let him get away with it.

AMPHITRYON (*to Sosia*)   Shut up! (*To Alcmena*) Now tell me: today, at the crack of dawn, I went away from you, did I?

ALCMENA (*shrugging*)   If it wasn't you two, then who told me the story of how the battle went?

AMPHITRYON (*flabbergasted*)   You mean to say you know about that?

ALCMENA   Of course! I heard from you all about how you stormed and took a great city and how you killed King Pterelas yourself.

AMPHITRYON (*as before*)   *I* told you that?

ALCMENA   Yes, you. And Sosia was there with us.

AMPHITRYON (*to Sosia*)   Did you hear me tell her all this today?

SOSIA (*with a how-silly-can-you-get tone of voice*)   Now where would I have heard you?

AMPHITRYON (*to Sosia, throwing up his hands*)   Ask *her*, not me.

ALCMENA (*to Amphitryon, witheringly*)   Strange, isn't it, that he won't contradict you.

AMPHITRYON   Sosia! Look at me.

SOSIA   I'm looking.

AMPHITRYON   Now, don't just yes me; I want you to tell me the truth. Did you hear me tell her today these things she said I did?

SOSIA (*scornfully*)   Please! Are you crazy too? Asking me a question like that! This is the first I've seen of her, just like yourself.

AMPHITRYON (*grimly*)   Well, Alcmena? Did you hear him?

ALCMENA (*calmly*)   I certainly did—telling lies!

AMPHITRYON   So you don't trust either him or your own husband, eh?

ALCMENA (*as before*)   Only because I trust myself most of all, and I know that everything happened exactly as I've told it to you.

AMPHITRYON   You say that I arrived here yesterday?

ALCMENA   You deny that you left here today?

AMPHITRYON (*exploding*)   Of course I do! I tell you, this is the first and only time I've been home!

ALCMENA (*tossing her head*)   Then I'd like to know whether you're also going to deny that this morning you gave me the gold cup you said you received as an award?

AMPHITRYON (*snorting*)   I did not give you that cup, nor did I mention a word about it! I'll admit I had in mind to give it to you, and I still do. (*Doing a double take*) Who told you about it, anyway?

ALCMENA (*coldly*)   You told me about it with your own lips and gave it to me with your own hands.

AMPHITRYON (*in desperation*)   Wait here. Don't move. Please! (*Turning and whispering to Sosia*) This is incredible, Sosia! How could she have known that I was awarded a gold cup? (*Menacingly*) Unless you met her before and told her the whole story.

SOSIA (*hastily*)   I never said a word to her! The first time I laid eyes on her was when you did.

AMPHITRYON (*clutching his head in despair*)   What kind of person is she!

ALCMENA (*patiently*)   Would you like me to show you the cup?

AMPHITRYON   Yes, I would!

ALCMENA Very well. (*She goes to the door and claps her hands. A moment later a maid appears in the doorway.*) Thessala, go back in and bring out the cup my husband gave me this morning.

AMPHITRYON (*pulling Sosia off to the side*) Come over here, Sosia. (*Sotto voce, nervously*) Listen, if she has that cup, that'll be the miracle to end all miracles.

SOSIA (*sotto voce, incredulously*) You mean you believe her? (*Pointing to a box in the hands of one of the porters*) But it's in this chest here. Locked and sealed with your own seal.

AMPHITRYON (*as before*) Is the seal intact?

SOSIA (*sotto voce*) Take a look.

AMPHITRYON (*doing so; sotto voce, relieved*) Perfect. Just the way I sealed it.

SOSIA (*sotto voce*) Listen, why don't you have her treated for lunacy?

AMPHITRYON (*sotto voce, gloomily*) Damn it all, I'll have to. She's crazy as a loon, damn it!

(*The maid reappears carrying a cup which she hands to Alcmena, who turns and calls to Amphitryon.*)

ALCMENA No need for any more talk. Here's your cup. (*Holding it up*) See?

AMPHITRYON (*striding over*) Let's have it.

ALCMENA (*handing it to him*) Here you are. And take a good look. Since you insist on denying cold facts, I'll make it as plain as day for you. (*Sternly*) Is this the cup that was awarded to you?

AMPHITRYON (*dumb struck*) In the name of Jove! What *is* this I see? It's the cup all right! (*To Sosia, dumbly*) Sosia, I'm a ruined man!

SOSIA (*grimly*) Either this woman is the greatest witch that ever lived, or your cup must still be in that box.

AMPHITRYON (*grimly*) Then hurry and open that box.

SOSIA (*throwing up his hands*)   Why bother? The seal's
still intact. (*Wildly*) Everything's working out perfectly:
you've produced a second Amphitryon, I've produced a
second Sosia, and now, if the cup comes up with a cup,
we've all become twins!

AMPHITRYON (*as before*)   We're opening that chest and having a look, and that's that!

SOSIA   Will you please just check the seal first, so you don't
start blaming me afterwards?

AMPHITRYON (*thundering*)   Open it! This woman wants to
drive us both insane with these stories of hers! (*Sosia
starts fumbling with the chest.*)

ALCMENA (*helplessly*)   Where would I have gotten it except from you? It was your gift to me!

AMPHITRYON (*grimly*)   I've got to look into this business.

SOSIA (*emitting a war whoop*)   By Jove! By Jove almighty!

AMPHITRYON (*startled*)   What's the matter?

SOSIA (*pointing to the chest, shaking like a leaf*)   There's no
cup in this chest!

AMPHITRYON   What's that you say?

SOSIA   The truth!

AMPHITRYON (*between his teeth*)   It better turn up, or
you'll pay for it with your hide.

ALCMENA (*holding out the cup, calmly*)   It has turned up—
here.

AMPHITRYON (*to Alcmena, as before*)   All right. Who gave
it to you?

ALCMENA (*as before*)   The man who's asking me the question.

SOSIA (*to Amphitryon, dancing with rage*)   Trying to trick
me, eh? You sneaked away from the ship, you ran ahead by
a different road, you took the cup out, you gave it to her,
and then you sneaked the seal back on!

AMPHITRYON (*clutching his head*)   Oh, my god! Are you

out to help this madwoman too? (*To Alcmena, wearily*)
So you say we arrived here yesterday?

ALCMENA (*quietly and calmly*)   Yes, I do. And the minute
you arrived, you greeted me. I greeted you and gave you a
kiss.

SOSIA (*to the audience, shaking his head dolefully*)   Right
away, I don't like the way it begins. Bad stuff, this kiss
business.

AMPHITRYON   Go on.

ALCMENA   Then you took a bath.

AMPHITRYON   And after my bath?

ALCMENA   You sat down to table.

SOSIA (*to Amphitryon*)   Good! Perfect! Get to the bottom of
this.

AMPHITRYON (*to Sosia, brusquely*)   Don't interrupt! (*To
Alcmena*) Go on with your story.

ALCMENA   Dinner was served. We ate together. I sat alongside you.

AMPHITRYON   On the same couch?

ALCMENA   On the same couch.

SOSIA (*shaking his head dolefully*)   I don't like the sound of
this dinner party!

AMPHITRYON (*turning on him*)   Let her go on with her ex-
planations. (*To Alcmena*) And after we finished dinner?

ALCMENA   You said you were sleepy. The table was cleared,
and we went off to bed.

AMPHITRYON   Where did you sleep?

ALCMENA   With you. In the same room. In the same bed.

AMPHITRYON (*gasping convulsively*)   You've done for me!

SOSIA (*in alarm*)   What's the matter?

AMPHITRYON   This woman's just murdered me!

ALCMENA (*agitated*)   What did I do? Please!

AMPHITRYON (*turning his back on her*)   Don't you talk to
me!

SOSIA What's the matter?

AMPHITRYON (*dramatically*) I'm ruined! Her honor—while I was away, it was stained!

ALCMENA (*wounded*) God in heaven! My dear husband, how can you say a thing like that about me!

AMPHITRYON (*wildly*) Your husband? I? Don't you call me by that name! False woman, it's a false name!

SOSIA (*to the audience, grinning*) This is a pretty sticky state of affairs if (*gesturing toward Amphitryon*) he's become a woman and isn't her man.

ALCMENA (*helplessly*) What did I do to make you say such things to me?

AMPHITRYON (*in a cold fury*) You've just presented the facts yourself. You have to ask *me* what you did wrong?

ALCMENA (*bewildered*) How could I have done anything wrong, when I was with you, the man I married?

AMPHITRYON (*screaming*) You were with me? (*To the world at large*) There isn't a woman alive as brazen as this one! (*Icily*) If you have no sense of shame, the very least you can do is act as if you did.

ALCMENA (*her eyes flashing*) Neither I nor anyone in my family would ever stoop to the behavior you're accusing me of. Is it your idea to catch me in adultery? You never will!

AMPHITRYON (*throwing up his arms in despair*) Oh, my god in heaven! (*Turning to Sosia*) Sosia, you at least recognize me, don't you?

SOSIA (*looking him over, coolly*) Just about.

AMPHITRYON Didn't I have dinner yesterday aboard ship in port?

ALCMENA (*coldly*) I have witnesses, too, to back up what *I* say.

SOSIA (*to Amphitryon, scratching his head*) I really don't know what to say about this whole business except that, maybe, there's some other Amphitryon who takes over your affairs while you're away and (*delicately, with a glance in*

Alcmena's direction) discharges your duties for you in your absence. If a fake Sosia is a miracle, believe you me, this other Amphitryon of yours is an even bigger one!

AMPHITRYON (*desperately*)   Some witch must have driven her out of her wits.

ALCMENA (*passionately*)   In the name of the supreme god of the heavens, in the name of Our Lady Juno, whom I reverence and worship with all my heart as I should, I swear to you that, outside of yourself, no man's body has touched mine to rob me of my honor!

AMPHITRYON (*dully*)   I only wish it were true.

ALCMENA (*resentfully*)   It *is* true. But that doesn't mean a thing because you don't want to believe it.

AMPHITRYON (*sneering*)   You're a woman, you're quick to swear.

ALCMENA (*proudly*)   A woman who's done no wrong can be quick to swear. She can speak up for herself with confidence and without fear.

AMPHITRYON (*muttering*)   You're quick to swear, all right.

ALCMENA (*as before*)   As any good woman should be!

AMPHITRYON (*as before*)   Good, eh? That's what you *say*.

ALCMENA (*gravely*)   What people generally mean by the word "dowry" is not what I consider my dowry to be. No—mine is decency and honor and self-control; respect for heaven, love for my parents, and good relations with all my family; to carry out your wishes, to give to the good, and to help the honest.

SOSIA   So help me, if everything she says is true, this woman's a paragon of virtue!

AMPHITRYON (*unhappily*)   I'm so mixed up, I don't even know my own name!

SOSIA (*promptly*)   You're Amphitryon, all right. But be careful: the way people have been changing ever since we got back, you might lose your right title to it if you don't watch out.

AMPHITRYON (*wearily*)   Alcmena, I must look into this matter, I can't just drop it.

ALCMENA   I'd be very glad if you would.

AMPHITRYON (*as before*)   Now what do you say to this? Your cousin Naucrates came over on the same ship with me. Suppose I bring him here from the dock. If he denies that things happened as you say they did, what do you think would be the fair thing to do? Can you give me any good reason why I shouldn't divorce you?

ALCMENA   None at all—*if* I've done something wrong.

AMPHITRYON   Agreed. (*To Sosia, gesturing toward the porters*) Take them inside. I'm going back to the ship to get Naucrates.

(*Amphitryon shuffles off despondently, stage right. Sosia gestures to the porters, who file into the house. He is about to follow them when, struck by a thought, he turns back to Alcmena.*)

SOSIA (*confidentially*)   Look, there's no one around now besides us two. Tell me the honest truth: is there another Sosia inside who looks exactly like me?

ALCMENA   Oh, get away from me! (*Disgustedly*) Like master, like man!

SOSIA (*grumbling*)   If that's the way you want it, I'll go. (*Enters the house.*)

ALCMENA (*to the audience, shaking her head sadly*)   A strange way for my husband to be acting. To get pleasure out of falsely accusing me of misconduct! (*Shrugging*) Well, whatever it is, I'll find out soon enough from Cousin Naucrates.

(*She turns and enters the house. The stage is now empty.*)

ACT III

(Enter Jove, stage left. He walks downstage and addresses the audience.)

JOVE I'm the Amphitryon with the servant Sosia who turns into Mercury when it's convenient, the Amphitryon who lives in *(pointing toward the sky)* the penthouse and sometimes becomes Jove when the spirit moves him. But the minute I arrive here, quick as a flash I change my clothes and become Amphitryon.

(With a respectful bow) This time I'm here for your sakes: I didn't want to leave this comedy only half done. At the same time, I wanted to come to Alcmena's rescue, since her husband, *(gesturing in the general direction of the port) that* Amphitryon, is accusing her of adultery though she's done nothing wrong. After all, I'd be to blame if what I alone was responsible for should fall on the head of poor, innocent Alcmena. *(Grinning)* I'll pass myself off now as Amphitryon, as I did before, and drive the whole household crazy. *(Becoming grave)* However, after it's all over, I'll reveal the secret, and I'll help Alcmena when her time comes: I'll see to it that she delivers both the child her husband conceived and the one I conceived with only one confinement and without any pain.

(Looking about) I told Mercury to stand by me immediately in case I had orders for him. *(With a wave of his hand, draws the audience's attention to the door of the house. The next second it opens, and Alcmena appears in the doorway.)* I'll speak to her right now.

(Alcmena emerges from her house carrying a bag. She slams the door shut behind her and, not noticing Jove, walks downstage and puts down the bag.)

ALCMENA *(to the audience, in a rage)* I simply can't stay in this house. To have my own husband accuse me this way of adultery, of shame and dishonor! Things that happened he shouts to high heaven never happened, and the next minute accuses me of things that never happened, that were none of my doing. What's more, he imagines I'll shrug all this off as just so much water under the bridge. I will not! He can't falsely accuse me of adultery—I won't stand for it! Either I leave him, or he gives me full satisfaction, and, what's more, swears to me that he takes back every word he's uttered against his wife's innocence!

JOVE (*to the audience*)   I'll have to arrange things the way she wants if I'm ever to get her to take back her fond lover. Amphitryon is an innocent victim: my doings have fallen on his neck, and my love affair let him in for a lot of trouble a little while ago. But now the tongue-lashing and cursing she got from him is falling on *my* neck, and *I'm* the innocent victim! (*Walks up to her.*)

ALCMENA (*to the audience*)   There's the man who's made his wife miserable by accusing her of shame and dishonor.

(*Turns her back on him as he comes up.*)

JOVE (*tenderly*)   My dear wife, I want to talk to you. Why do you turn your back on me?

ALCMENA (*furiously*)   It's my nature. I can't stand the sight of an enemy.

JOVE   Hey, what's this! An enemy?

ALCMENA (*as before*)   Exactly. It's the truth—unless you're ready to accuse me of calling you by a false name this time too!

JOVE (*putting his arm about her; meltingly*)   You're so angry!

ALCMENA (*thrusting his arm away*)   You keep your hands off me! (*Witheringly*) After all, if you had any sense and were in your right mind, you'd hardly want to hold a conversation, serious or otherwise, with a woman you consider and call immoral. Not unless you're stupider than the stupidest!

JOVE (*earnestly*)   My calling you so doesn't make you any more so, and I *don't* consider you immoral. I've come here for only one purpose: to apologize to you. I've never felt so badly about anything as I did when I heard you were angry with me. "Why did you say such things?" you'll ask. I'll tell you why. It was not, I swear it, that I thought you were immoral; I was just testing your feelings, what you'd do, how you'd be inclined to take it. What I said to you before wasn't serious—it was all a joke! Just ask Sosia.

ALCMENA (*glaring at him*)   You go ahead and bring my Cousin Naucrates, just as you said you were going to do, to be your witness that you hadn't been here before.

JOVE (*reproachfully*)   Now, if something's said in a joke, it's not fair to take it seriously.

ALCMENA (*bitterly*)   A joke that cut me to the very heart, as I know only too well.

JOVE (*on his knees*)   Alcmena, I beg you! On my knees! Please! Forgive me! Pardon me! Don't be angry with me!

ALCMENA (*coldly*)   My character makes everything you've said against me simply meaningless. (*Turning from him*) Since I've never had anything to do with immorality in deed, I want nothing to do with it in word. I'm saying good-by now. Keep your part of the property, and arrange to return mine. And now, if you please, send some servants to escort me.

JOVE (*frantically*)   Are you in your right mind?

ALCMENA (*picking up her bag, as before*)   If you won't send any, I'll go by myself. (*Proudly*) My honor will be my escort! (*Starts walking away.*)

JOVE (*urgently*)   Wait! (*As she stops*) I will swear any oath you want that I believe you are a faithful wife. (*Dramatically*) And if I swear falsely, (*raising his eyes to heaven*) Almighty Jove, I call on you to bring heaven's wrath upon Amphitryon for all time!

ALCMENA (*shuddering*)   No! Heaven's blessing!

JOVE (*dryly*)   I'm sure it will be that, because that was no

false oath I gave you. (*Taking her gently by the arm*)
Now, are you still angry with me?

ALCMENA (*reluctantly*)   No.

JOVE   Good! (*Gently*) You know, in life things like this happen all the time. We have our joys, and then again our
sorrows. We have fights, and then we make up again. Yet,
whenever we have fights of this kind and make up again,
we're twice as good friends as we were before.

ALCMENA (*reproachfully*)   You should have been careful
and not said such a thing in the first place. (*Smiling
at him*) But, since you've apologized completely for everything, well, I'll let it go.

(*They embrace and stand for a moment smiling happily at
each other.*)

JOVE (*as if suddenly remembering something*)   Listen, you
must have the ritual utensils made ready for me. When I
was at the front I made some vows about what I'd do if I
returned safe and sound, and I want to carry them out.

ALCMENA   I'll take care of it. (*Claps her hands, and two maid
servants appear at the door.*)

JOVE (*to the servants*)   Call Sosia out here. (*They re-enter
the house. He turns to Alcmena.*) I want him to bring
Blepharo—he was captain of my ship—here to have lunch
with me. (*To the audience, grinning*) Blepharo is not only
going to get no lunch—he's going to be one surprised man
when I haul Amphitryon out of here by the neck!

ALCMENA (*to the audience*)   I wonder what he's up to, talking to himself like that? (*Her attention caught, glances toward the door*) Someone's coming out. It's Sosia.

(*Sosia emerges from the house and walks up to Jove.*)

SOSIA (*to Jove, seriously*)   Here I am, Amphitryon. Anything
to be done, just say the word and I'll do it.

JOVE   Sosia, you've come just at the right time.

SOSIA (*looking from the one to the other*)   Have you two

made peace? (*Breaking into a smile*) Well, I'm delighted!
It's a pleasure to see you two relaxed! (*Seriously again*)
The system a good servant should follow is this: whatever
your owners do, you do, you take your expression from
them. If they're sad, you be sad; if they're gay, you be gay.
(*Switching on the smile again*) So, tell me: you've made
up, have you?

JOVE (*eying him piercingly*) What are you making jokes
for? You know very well everything I said a while back
was just in fun.

SOSIA (*bewildered*) Just in fun was it? I thought you were
dead serious!

JOVE (*smiling at Alcmena*) I've apologized for everything,
and now there's peace between us.

SOSIA Fine!

JOVE And now I want to go in and take care of those vows
I made.

SOSIA Good idea.

JOVE You go to the pier and invite Captain Blepharo to
lunch for me. We'll eat just as soon as I'm done with my
prayers.

SOSIA (*over his shoulder as he dashes off, stage right*) By the
time you think I've just arrived there, I'll already be back
here.

JOVE (*calling after him*) Just hurry back.

ALCMENA You don't want me for anything, do you? Then
I'll go in and get ready whatever you need.

JOVE You run along and get everything set up as quickly
as you can.

ALCMENA You can come in whenever you want. I'll see to
it there are no delays.

JOVE (*kissing her tenderly*) That's the way an attentive wife
should talk. (*She goes into the house, and he turns to the
audience.*) I fooled them both, mistress and servant. They
think I'm Amphitryon—are they ever wrong! (*Looking*

upward) Hey there! You, the immortal Sosia! Put in an appearance here. You hear what I say even though you're not here in the flesh. When Amphitryon gets back, keep him away from the house. Use any trick you can think of. I want you to play around with him till I've had my pleasure with this wife of his I'm borrowing. Now, please see that you do all this just the way you know I want it done. And I want you to stand by and help while I (*grinning*) offer up prayers to myself!

(*He enters the house. A moment later Mercury dashes in at top speed, stage left.*)

SONG

MERCURY (*yelling*)

> Hey, gangway everyone, clear the road! Out of my way, I say!
>
> No man alive better have the nerve to stand and block my way!

(*Pulling up, in normal tones*)

> Why shouldn't the right to threaten the public be given gods, like me,
>
> When two-bit slaves do it all the time, in every comedy?
> They rush to yell, "The boat's come in! Your father's home, and mad!"
>
> But *I'm* obeying Jove himself; I'm here on orders from Dad.
> So *I've* an even greater right to holler "Clear the way"—
> My father calls and, quick, I run; one word, and I obey.
> With Jove I'm just as dutiful as any father's pet.
>
> When he's in love, I'm Helpful Henry; I aid, advise, abet,
> And share his joys—the times he's happy are when I'm happiest.
>
> He has affairs. That's good. He's smart: he does as he likes best.
>
> And everyone of you should too—of course, with moderation.
>
> Now, Father wants Amphitryon fooled. You'll see a presentation,

A spectacle for spectators, of fooling at its height.
I'll put a garland on my head, and make believe I'm tight,
Then climb to the roof and, when he comes, get rid of him
    from there:
Though he hasn't had a drop to drink, he'll end up soused
    for fair.

(*Chuckling*)

And then his servant Sosia will pay for what I've done—
Amphitryon will demonstrate that *he's* the guilty one.
What's that to me? My job is Jove, to be at his beck and
    call.

(*His attention caught, he looks off, stage right*)

Well, look who's here—Amphitryon. May I kindly ask you
    all
To give me your attention while I take him for a ride.
It involves my acting out a part, so now I'll go inside
And fix myself to look as though I'd tied one on some-
    where.
Then up I go to the top of the roof to drive him off from
    there.

(*Mercury dashes inside. A moment later Amphitryon enters, shuffling along disconsolately.*)

AMPHITRYON · (*to the audience, irritably*) I went to get
Naucrates, but I couldn't. He wasn't on the ship, he wasn't
at home, and I wasn't able to find a soul in town who had
seen him. I've been all over: up and down every street, in
the gyms, in the drugstores, the bazaar, the market, the
athletic field, the main square, all the doctors' offices, all the
barbers', every temple in town—I'm worn out with looking,
and I can't find him any place.

    (*Falls silent a moment, shaking his head bitterly. Then,
resolutely*) I'll go home, get Alcmena, and go further into
this matter of who it was who made her disgrace herself.
I'm going to get to the bottom of this business or die in the
attempt!

    (*Strides up to the door, tries it, and steps back in sur-*

prise) The door's bolted! (*Bitterly*) Great! Just like everything else that's been going on around here. Well, I'll just bang on it. (*Pounding away*) Open up! Hey, isn't anyone going to open this door?

(*Mercury suddenly appears on the roof, a garland sitting askew on his head, and leans over.*)

MERCURY (*as if drunk*)   Who'z 'at at the door?

AMPHITRYON (*shouting*)   I am.

MERCURY (*with drunken incomprehension*)   Wha' d'ya mean, "I am?"

AMPHITRYON (*snarling*)   You heard me!

MERCURY (*waggling a finger at him, playfully reproachful*) Breaking down doors this way! God will punish you.

AMPHITRYON (*taken aback, incredulously*)   What's that?

MERCURY (*piously*)   It's that He'll make you unhappy your whole life long.

AMPHITRYON (*recognizing the face, in a voice of thunder*) Sosia!

MERCURY (*brightly*)   That's right. I'm Sosia. (*Belligerently*) Think I'd forgotten it? What do you want?

AMPHITRYON (*dancing with rage*)   You good-for-nothing, you have to *ask* me what I want?

MERCURY (*belligerently*)   Sure, I'm asking. You almost banged that door off its hinges, dumbbell. You think the government supplies us with doors? What are you looking at me for, stupid? What do you want? Who are you, anyway?

AMPHITRYON (*between his teeth*)   God damn you, you'll be the death of every whip I own! Asking me who I am! I'll warm your god-damned hide for you for talking like that!

MERCURY (*sadly*)   You must have been a bad boy when you were young.

AMPHITRYON   How so?

MERCURY   Because, in your old age, you're begging for a beating.

(*Roars at his own joke.*)

AMPHITRYON   (*between his teeth*)   I'll torture the life out of you for those words.

MERCURY   (*piously*)   I'm going to pray for you.

AMPHITRYON   How's that?

MERCURY   I'm going to pray you come to a bad end.

[At this point there was a large gap, perhaps three hundred verses, in the lost manuscript from which all our surviving copies of the *Amphitryon* derive. However, from some twenty random lines cited in ancient grammars and similar works, we can reconstruct what took place. Mercury dumps a bucket of water on Amphitryon, and the slapstick between them continues until the noise draws Alcmena out of the house; whereupon she and Amphitryon renew their quarrel. At some point Sosia enters; he had carried out Jove's orders, and has Captain Blepharo in tow. Amphitryon, of course, immediately wades into Sosia, but Jove appears on the scene, disguised as Amphitryon, and wades into *him*, accusing him of lechery and seduction. The argument between them grows hot and heavy, each claiming that he is the real thing and the other an impostor, until both agree to put the problem in Blepharo's hands: he is to test them and decide. Blepharo makes a number of attempts, gets nowhere, and, at the point where he admits defeat, the text resumes. Jove, Amphitryon, and Blepharo are on stage; we are now in Act IV.]

BLEPHARO   Look—you two divide yourselves up by yourselves. I'm leaving, I've got things to do. (*Shaking his head*) I don't think I've ever seen anything as queer as all this anywhere.

AMPHITRYON   (*desperately*)   Blepharo, I beg you: stand by me; don't go away!

BLEPHARO   (*resolutely*)   Good-by! What's the good of my

standing by if I can't tell which one of you to stand by?
(*Leaves, stage right, still shaking his head.*)

JOVE (*to the audience, excitedly*)   I'm going into the house.
Alcmena's giving birth! (*Turns and rushes inside.*)

AMPHITRYON (*to the audience, watching Blepharo go off and
not noticing Jove's departure*)   Oh, my god! Now what do
I do? My friends and allies have all run out on me!
(*Grimly*) By god, he's not going to make a fool of me like
this and get away with it, whoever he is! I'm going straight
to King Creon this minute and tell him about the whole
business. I'll get even on that witch doctor who's turned
my whole household into lunatics. (*Turning to carry out his
threat and seeing no one; startled*) Where is he? By god,
I'll bet he's inside, with my wife! (*Clutching his head*) I'll
swear, not another man in all Thebes has such misery! Now
what do I do? Nobody knows who I am. Everybody plays
any joke he feels like on me. (*Wildly*) I'll break into the
house, that's what I'll do. Anyone I lay eyes on—maid or
servant, wife or seducer, my own father or grandfather—
I'll cut their throats right there in the house! All the gods
in heaven, including Jove himself, can't stop me even if
they want to. I've made up my mind and I'm going to do
it! Here I go into the house!

(*He makes a mad dash for the door but a sudden tremendous clap of thunder and blinding flash of lightning stop him
dead in his tracks; he falls flat on the ground, unconscious.*)

ACT V

(*Amphitryon is still unconscious, sprawled full length on the ground in front of his house. The thunder and lightning continue for a few moments and then gradually cease. Suddenly the door flies open, and Bromia, Alcmena's maid, her hair disheveled and her clothes in disarray, bursts out. Without noticing Amphitryon, she rushes downstage and addresses the audience.*)

SONG

BROMIA (*hysterically*)

My mind has given up the thought that I've any chance to survive,

My heart's abandoned every hope—I'll never stay alive!

It seems to me that everything—the earth, the air, the sky—

Have all conspired against my life, have willed to see me die.

The strangest things went on in the house! God knows what I should do!

(*Gasping for breath*)

Oh, god! I'm sick! Some water, please! My end is near, I'm through!

My head aches so, my hearing's gone, my vision's not what it should be.

No other woman's this miserable, no other ever *could* be!

(*Stops, gets hold of herself, and resumes much more calmly.*)

It's what Alcmena had happen to her. Once in labor, she prayed to god.

Then, bang and crash! Thunder and lightning! So sudden, so near, so hard!

The sound knocked over all of us; we fell in our tracks, struck dumb.

And then a mighty voice called out, "Alcmena, help has come!

Don't fear! A god from heaven's on hand to shed his favor
    on thee."
"And rise, all you," it said to us, "who fell through fear of
    me."
I rose, since I had fallen too. The lightning gleamed so, I
Was sure our house had caught on fire. Then I heard
    Alcmena's cry.
For a moment, horror held me fast—but fear for her won
    out.
I ran to see what she'd called me for. Amazed, I look about:
She'd given birth to twins, two boys. It was all a mystery,
A birth none saw or had foreseen.

(*Suddenly noticing Amphitryon*)

         My god, what's this I see?
Who is the gentleman stretched out here, before our very
    door!
Some victim of Jove's thunderbolt? By Jove, he looks it, for
He's laid out there as if he's dead. I think I'd better run
And check. Perhaps I know the man.

(*Rushing up to Amphitryon and taking a look; startled*)

         My master, Amphitryon!

(*Shouting in his ear*)

Amphitryon!

AMPHITRYON (*groaning*)
 I'm dead.

BROMIA

      Get up!

AMPHITRYON (*as before*)

        A corpse.

BROMIA (*reaching out and taking his hand*)

         Here, let me have your hand.

AMPHITRYON (*feebly*)
 Who's holding me?

BROMIA

      Your Bromia.

(*She hauls mightily and succeeds in pulling him to his feet.*)

AMPHITRYON (*holding his head, his eyes closed; dazedly*)

But *I* don't understand—

That crack from Jove has me numb with fear. I feel as if I died

And have just come back from the underworld.

(*Finally pulling out of his stupor and looking at her curiously*)

But what brings *you* outside?

BROMIA (*nervously*)

The same fear and dread gripped all of us.

(*Pointing to the door; dramatically*)

In there, the house where you dwell,

I saw such a wonder I'm still unnerved.

(*Covering her face, hysterically*)

Amphitryon, it's hell!

AMPHITRYON (*pulling her hands from her face and forcing her to look at him*)

Now answer this: am I your master? Am I Amphitryon?

BROMIA

Of course you are.

AMPHITRYON

No, look again.

BROMIA (*as before*)

Of course you're Amphitryon.

AMPHITRYON (*to the world at large, bitterly*)

The only one of my household here who's preserved her sanity.

BROMIA (*reproachfully*)

No sir, we're all completely sane.

AMPHITRYON (*as before*)

There's one exception—me.

The shameful conduct of my wife has driven *me* insane.

BROMIA (*passionately*)

But you, yourself, will admit you're wrong as soon as I explain!

(Stops for a moment to make sure he is willing to listen, then continues gently) Yes, you'll realize that your wife is a decent and honorable woman. It will take me only a moment to tell you some things that will prove it beyond any doubt.

(She pauses, then begins again, observing him keenly to note the effect of her words.) To begin with, Alcmena has just given birth to twins, two boys.

AMPHITRYON *(blankly)*   Twins, you say?

BROMIA   Twins.

AMPHITRYON *(hopelessly)*   God help me!

BROMIA *(impatiently)*   Please let me go on—I want to show you that god *is* helping both you and your wife.

AMPHITRYON   Go on.

BROMIA *(excitedly)*   When her time came, and she went into labor, your wife, as women in childbirth always do, washed her hands, covered her head, and prayed to god to help her. The next second, there was a mighty clap of thunder. At first we all thought your house would come crashing down; the lightning gleamed so, the whole place looked as though it were made of gold.

AMPHITRYON *(savagely)*   Will you kindly let me go as soon as you're through having fun with me? *(Shrugs as Bromia gestures helplessly and falls silent)* All right, what happened next?

BROMIA *(resuming excitedly)*   During all this, not one of us heard your wife utter a groan or a cry. It was a completely painless delivery.

AMPHITRYON *(grudgingly)*   Well, I'm glad to hear that—in spite of all she's done to me.

BROMIA *(impatiently)*   Forget all that and just listen to what I'm going to tell you. *(Resuming her excited narrative tone)* When it was all over, she told us to wash the babies down.

We started right in. Well, I can't tell you how big and strong the baby was that I was bathing! There wasn't one of us who could pin the diapers and clothes around him.

AMPHITRYON *(scratching his head)* This is an incredible story. If it's true, my wife certainly received a lot of help from heaven.

BROMIA *(eagerly)* Believe me, what comes next you'll say is even more incredible. *(Resuming her narrative tone)* I had just put him in his cradle when there slithered down through the skylight two serpents with crests, both of them simply enormous. The next minute, there they were, the two of them, with heads raised looking about.

AMPHITRYON *(shuddering)* Oh, my god!

BROMIA *(reassuringly)* Nothing to be afraid about. *(Resuming her narrative tone)* The serpents eyed everyone there. As soon as they spotted the children, they made a rush for them. I pulled the cradles back and steered them away; I was frightened for myself but even more afraid for the babies. The snakes followed after, fiercer than ever. Then that child, the one I had bathed, saw them. He jumped right out of his cradle, went straight for them, and, in a flash, had one gripped in each hand.

AMPHITRYON Incredible! This is a very dangerous deed you've described! Just hearing about it gives me the shudders! What then? Go on?

BROMIA The baby strangled both those serpents. And, while he was doing it, a mighty voice was heard calling to Alcmena—

AMPHITRYON *(interrupting angrily)* Who was the man?

BROMIA Man? It was the lord of men and of gods, almighty Jove! He announced that he had had intercourse with Alcmena in secret and that the child that had killed the snakes was his. *(As an afterthought)* The other, he said was yours.

(For a full moment Amphitryon stands buried in thought.)

AMPHITRYON (*suddenly his old vibrant self*) Well, I certainly have no cause for complaint when I'm given the chance to share my goods with Jove. Go inside and have the ritual utensils made ready for me right away. I want to pray hard and long, and beg almighty Jove for peace. And I'll call in Tiresias, the prophet, and ask what he thinks I should do. At the same time I'll tell him how this whole business happened. (*A tremendous clap of thunder is heard.*) What's that? Thunder—but so loud! (*Falling to his knees*) Oh god, help me, please!

VOICE FROM OFF STAGE (*slowly and impressively*) Take heart, Amphitryon. I am here to help you and your family. There is nothing to be afraid of. Prophets, fortune tellers—don't bother with any of them. I will tell you both the future and the past much better than they, for I am Jove.

To begin with, I borrowed your Alcmena's body, slept with her, and conceived a son by her. You too conceived a son, when you left to go to the front. She has brought forth both together, in one birth. The one sprung from my seed will do deeds that will make your name great forever. Go back now to Alcmena and live with her in the harmony you two have always known. She deserves no reproaches; *I* forced her to do what she did. And now I must return to the heavens.

AMPHITRYON I'll do as you command—but I beg you: don't forget your promises. I'll go inside now to my wife, and I won't bother with Tiresias. (*He rises from his knees, walks downstage and addresses the audience.*) And now, ladies and gentlemen, for Jove's sake, a good loud round of applause!

THE POT OF GOLD

DRAMATIS PERSONAE

EUCLIO, *an elderly gentleman, not very well off, father of Phaedria*

GRAPE (STAPHYLA), *his aged housekeeper (slave)*

EUNOMIA, *an elderly, well-to-do lady, sister of Megadorus and mother of Lyconides*

MEGADORUS, *an elderly, well-to-do gentleman, brother of Eunomia and uncle of Lyconides*

STROBILUS, *his servant (slave)*

EEL (CONGRIO), *a cook (slave)*

CHARCOAL (ANTHRAX), *a cook (slave)*

PYTHODICUS, *a servant belonging to Megadorus' household (slave)*

STROBILUS, *servant of Lyconides*

LYCONIDES, *a young man about town, son of Eunomia and nephew of Megadorus*

[PHRYGIA, *a piper (slave)*]

[ELEUSIUM, *a piper (slave)*]

[PHAEDRIA, *a lovely young girl, daughter of Euclio*]

SERVANTS

SCENE

A street in Athens. Three buildings front on it: the house of Euclio, the house of Megadorus, and the Temple of Trust; the last has an altar in front of it. The exit on stage left leads downtown, that on stage right to the country.

PROLOGUE

(The door of Euclio's house opens, and a wraithlike little figure flutters out and proceeds downstage to deliver the prologue.)

SPIRIT OF EUCLIO'S HOUSE   In case you're wondering who I am, I'll take a second to explain. (*Gesturing toward Euclio's door*) This house you just saw me come out of—well, I'm the special spirit assigned to the family there. I've been living in the house for years; I took care of it for the grandfather and the father of the man who lives there now.

Now, the grandfather enlisted my help and, without letting a soul know, put in my charge a treasure of gold; he buried it in the middle of the fireplace and begged me to watch over it for him. To his dying day he didn't want his son to know about it; he had such a miserly soul he preferred to leave the poor man a pauper rather than show him where this money was. All he left was some farmland, not very much at that, and, with a lot of hard work, his son managed to make a miserable living out of it.

When he died—I mean the one who put the gold in my charge—I began watching to see whether the son would show more respect for me than his father had. But he took less and less notice of me as time went on, and paid me less and less respect. (*Grinning*) So I returned the favor—and he died too.

He left behind a son, the man living here now, who's the same sort as his father and grandfather. However, he has an only daughter who never fails, every day of the year, to offer me incense, wine, or the like, and set out fresh flowers for me. To repay her for this high regard, I saw to it that Euclio discovered the money. I did it to make it easier for him to get her married if he wanted to.

You see, a boy from one of the best families has seduced her. The boy knows who the girl he seduced is, but she doesn't know who her seducer was—and her father doesn't know she's been seduced!

(*Leaning forward and speaking confidentially*) Today I'll arrange to have (*gesturing towards Megadorus' house*) this old fellow next door ask to marry her. I have a special reason for doing this: (*nodding knowingly*) it's going to make it easier for her seducer to marry her. Now, the old fellow who'll ask for her hand is the uncle of the boy who did her wrong. It all happened in the dark during the all-night festival for Lady Ceres. (*Suddenly angry shouting is heard from inside Euclio's house.*) There's the old man hollering his head off as usual. He's throwing the old hag out of the house so she won't find out his secret. I think he wants to take a look at his gold to make sure it hasn't been stolen.

ACT I

(*The shouts from inside grow louder. A second later, the door flies open, and an old woman bursts out with an old man at her heels. As they do, the Spirit slips unobserved back into the house.*

The old woman is Grape [Staphyla, *literally "grape cluster," presumably so-called because of a weakness for the jug*], *a wretched old hag who is Euclio's only servant. The old man is Euclio, "good reputation." He is dressed in the simple, threadbare clothes of a poor man. At the moment he is in a rage, but this is the result of an emotional state not something innate in his character; under normal circumstances he is no more irascible than any other poor man.*)

EUCLIO (*roaring*) Out! Out, I say! God damn it, I want you out of here, you pry-eyed spy in petticoats, you!

GRAPE (*whining*) What are you beating up a poor old woman like me for?

EUCLIO (*savagely*) To keep you a poor old woman. And to make a worthless slut live the way a worthless slut should.

GRAPE (*helplessly*) But why throw me out of the house now?

EUCLIO So, you damned slut, I'm supposed to give you reasons, am I? (*Pointing to a spot well away from the house*) Over there, away from the door! OVER THERE! (*Impatiently, as the old woman hobbles along*) Look at her dawdle! Do you know what's going to happen to you? I swear to god, if I get a club or a whip in my hands, I'll put some speed in that snail's pace of yours!

GRAPE (*to herself, bitterly*) I wish to god I could be sent to the gallows! Better than slaving for you and having to live like this.

EUCLIO (*to himself, snarling*) Aha! The sneak's whispering secrets to herself. (*To Grape*) So help me I'll gouge the eyes out of your head—that'll keep you from spying on

what I'm doing! (*As Grape stops*) Keep moving! Farther.
Still farther. Whoa—stand there. If you budge the width of
my little finger from that spot, or turn around, until I tell
you to, by god I'll send you to the hangman to learn how
to behave. (*To the audience, nervously*) I swear, never in
all my life have I laid eyes on a worse old hag than this
one. I'm scared stiff of her—she might trap me with some
trick when I'm not on my guard and find out where the
money's hidden. She's got eyes in the back of her head,
damn her. I'll go in now and check whether the money's
where I hid it. (*Tearing his hair*) My god, my god, the
worry that money gives me! (*Goes into the house.*)

GRAPE (*to the audience, shaking her head in perplexity*) My
goodness, I don't know what I can say to explain the terrible
thing that's happened to Euclio, what kind of madness this
is. Imagine—throwing a poor woman out of the house this
way ten times a day! I simply can't understand what this
lunacy is that's come over him. All night long he doesn't
close his eyes, and then, when dawn comes, all day long
he sits in the house like a crippled shoemaker.

  (*Pauses for a second, then throws her arms wide in
desperation.*) And I really don't know what I can do now
to hide his daughter's disgrace—the time for her to have
her baby is getting very near. (*Heaving a sigh*) If you
ask me, the best thing I can do is put a rope around my
neck and hang myself till I become one long, limp capital I!

(*She stops suddenly as the door flies open and Euclio
steps out again. It is immediately apparent that his state of
mind is much improved.*)

EUCLIO (*to the audience*)   Finally I can leave the house with
my mind at ease. I've had a look, and everything inside is
safe. (*To Grape*) Go back in the house now and keep an
eye on things inside.

GRAPE (*with heavy sarcasm*)   Oh, sure. I'm to keep an eye
on things inside, am I? So nobody will walk off with the
house, I suppose. Because there's nothing else there that

would do a thief any good—all we've got is plenty of nothing and spider webs.

EUCLIO (*with equal sarcasm*)   I'm surprised the good lord
doesn't turn me into the Shah of Persia or Alexander the
Great just for your benefit, you old bitch. (*Roaring*) I
want you to keep an eye on those spider webs for me!

(*Glares at her a moment and then resumes more calmly*)
I'm a poor man. I admit it, I put up with it. What god
gives, I bear. Now go inside and keep the door shut; I'll be
back soon. Watch out that you don't let any strangers in
the house. And I want you to put out the fire: someone
may want a light, and I don't want to give them any excuse
to ask you for it. (*Grimly*) If I see that fire still alive, I'll
put out *you*, and fast. If anyone asks for water, tell him
our bucket ran away. Knife, ax, pestle, mortar, the things
neighbors are always asking to borrow—say we had a robbery and everything was stolen. I absolutely forbid a single
soul to be allowed in my house while I'm away. I'm warning you—if Lady Luck herself comes to the door, you're not
to let her in.

GRAPE (*muttering*)   If you ask me, she'll take good care not
to come, on her own. She's never visited *our* house, even
when she's been in the neighborhood.

EUCLIO   Shut up and go in.

GRAPE (*promptly*)   I'm shutting up and going in. (*She goes
inside.*)

EUCLIO (*calling after her*)   Shut the door tight and double-
lock it. I'll be back soon.

(*Turning to the audience*) It's sheer torture to leave the
house. Believe me, I hate to go off. But I know what I'm
doing. You see, our ward leader announced that a cash
bonus of ten dollars a man was going to be distributed. If
I pass mine up and don't claim it, I have the feeling everybody will immediately suspect I have money in the house.
Ten dollars isn't much, but people don't expect a poor man
to turn up his nose at it and not bother to collect it. (*Shaking his head worriedly*) As it is, in spite of all I do to keep

everybody from knowing, everybody seems to know. Everybody gives me a much more friendly hello than they used to. They come to me, stop, shake my hand, ask me about my health, what I'm doing, how things are going . . . (*Stands in preoccupied silence for a moment. Then, rousing himself*) Well, I'll be on my way. Afterwards, I'll get myself back home just as fast as I can!

(*He leaves, stage left, and the stage is now empty.*)

ACT II

*(Enter Eunomia and Megadorus from Megadorus' house.
Megadorus, "big giver," is a pleasant old gentleman,
dressed expensively and in good taste, who gives an unmis-
takable impression of honesty and decency. Eunomia, "proper
rules," his older sister, is a proper, serious Athenian matron.)*

SONG

EUNOMIA

> I do hope, my brother, you'll feel that what I say
> To you, I'm saying as a sister should—
> My words are from the heart and for your good.
> And I don't deceive myself one bit: I know
> The name we women have for making trouble.
> We're all considered chatterboxes, and
> It's true. There's never been, so men impute,
> A single case on record of a female mute.
> Despite this, brother, keep one thing in mind,
> That you are my nearest of kin and I am yours.
> And so it's only right for both of us
> To think about and advise—I you, you me—
> Whatever we feel is best for each other's good,
> And not to keep this back or be afraid
> To say it. You should share your thoughts with me,
> And I no less should share all mine with you.
> That's why just now I sneaked you out of doors—
> To discuss an important personal matter of yours.

MEGADORUS *(smiling broadly and reaching out his hand)*

> My good woman, come here. I want to shake your
> hand.

EUNOMIA *(with a great show of looking puzzled)*

> Where is she? Who *is* this good woman. I don't under-
> stand.

MEGADORUS

> It's you.

EUNOMIA (*as before*)
   Who, me?

MEGADORUS (*gallantly—but with a mischievous gleam in his eye*)
      Don't say I'm wrong because
I'll say that *you're* wrong.

EUNOMIA (*playfully*)
       Ah, don't break the laws
Of truth. You see, you can't pick out, dear brother,
 A woman who's good. Each one is worse than the
  other.

MEGADORUS (*nodding vigorously*)
Rest assured, I'll never contest the point. I agree!

EUNOMIA (*darting a sharp look at him but, reassured by his deadpan serenity, getting down to business*)
Your attention, please.

MEGADORUS (*promptly*)
     It's all yours. Just order me,
And whatever you want, you count on it, I'll do.

EUNOMIA
There's something that I consider best for you,
And to talk you into it, is why I'm here.

MEGADORUS (*dryly*)
You're always doing this for me, my dear.

EUNOMIA (*smugly*)
I think I should.

MEGADORUS
    What is it?

EUNOMIA (*enthusiastically*)
      To guarantee
A life of joy and raise a family—

MEGADORUS (*interrupting, fervently*)
  God grant it all!

EUNOMIA (*ignoring the interruption*)
     —I'd like to see
You take a wife.

MEGADORUS (*clapping a hand to his brow, roaring*)
> You've murdered me!

EUNOMIA (*alarmed*)
> What's happened?

MEGADORUS
> > You just bashed in my head!
> > Those words you said were heavy as lead!

EUNOMIA (*as if addressing a schoolboy*)
> Come, do as sister says.

MEGADORUS
> > You'd like me to?
>
> All right.

EUNOMIA (*earnestly*)
> > I'm sure it's just the thing for you.

MEGADORUS
> And I'd prefer committing suicide.
> Any girl you care to pick I'll make my bride
> Upon these terms: she comes tomorrow for the
>   marriage;
> Next day she leaves in the undertaker's carriage.
> With this condition, I'll take the girl you say.
> Let's have her, and you name the wedding day.

EUNOMIA (*blithely ignoring her brother's remonstrances,
thoughtfully*)
> I can give you one whose dowry's huge, but then
> She's rather old, she'll never see fifty again.

(*Brightly*)
> But if you say to go and ask her for you,
> I assure you, brother, I'm perfectly willing to.

MEGADORUS (*patiently*)   Do you mind if I ask you a question?

EUNOMIA (*as before*)   Not at all! Ask any you want.

MEGADORUS   Let's say a man past middle age takes a middle-aged wife, and, by some luck, the old gentleman gets the old girl pregnant. Don't you agree that there's a perfect name all ready for their offspring—Postumus?[1] (*Stops to observe the reaction and, there being none, continues.*) Now, my sister, I'm going to spare you a lot of this trouble you're going to. Thanks to heaven and the family fortune, I have money enough. I don't need your high and mighty ladies with their big dowries, their shouting, ordering, fancy carriages, silks and satins. They simply spend a husband into slavery.

EUNOMIA (*stiffly*)   Then would you please tell me who it is you would like to marry?

MEGADORUS (*looking her straight in the eye*)   All right, I will. Do you know old Euclio? The neighbor next door, who's not very well off?

EUNOMIA   I do. And a very nice man too, I must say.

MEGADORUS (*as before*)   I'd like to make his daughter my wife. (*As Eunomia opens her mouth*) Not a word! I know what you're going to say: she's a pauper. Well, this particular pauper pleases me.

EUNOMIA (*shrugging*)   God bless the marriage.

MEGADORUS (*cheerfully*)   Just what I hope.

EUNOMIA (*having lost interest*)   I must be off now.

MEGADORUS   Good-by.

EUNOMIA   Good-by. (*Exit, stage left.*)

MEGADORUS (*to himself*)   I'll have a talk with Euclio, if he's home. (*Turns and happens to look toward the wings, stage left.*) Ah, there he is. Must be on his way back from someplace.

(*Enter Euclio stomping along in a foul temper.*)

EUCLIO (*muttering to himself*)   I had the feeling I was going for nothing when I left the house; that's why I hated to go. (*Bitterly*) Not one of the members of the ward council showed up, and neither did the leader, who was supposed

---

[1] A name commonly given to a son born after the father has died.

to distribute the bonus. Now I'm in a hurry to hurry home
—my head's here but my heart's in the house.

MEGADORUS (*effusively*)   Well, Euclio! The very best wishes
to you, my friend!

EUCLIO (*looking up in surprise, warily*)   The very best to
you too, Megadorus.

MEGADORUS (*solicitously*)   Tell me, how're you feeling? All
right? As well as you'd like?

EUCLIO (*to the audience, worried*)   When a rich man's so
nice to somebody poor, there's something behind it. That
fellow knows I've got gold; that's the reason for these extra-
nice greetings I'm getting.

MEGADORUS (*as before*)   You say you're feeling well?

EUCLIO (*looking woebegone*)   When it comes to money, not
well at all, believe me.

MEGADORUS (*heartily*)   Well, if your mind's at peace, you've
got all you need to enjoy life.

EUCLIO (*to the audience, agonized*)   I'll swear the old hag's
tipped him off about the gold! Absolutely no doubt about
it! (*Between his teeth*) Wait till I get back inside! I'll cut
her tongue off and gouge her eyes out!

MEGADORUS (*puzzled*)   What are you talking to yourself
about?

EUCLIO (*quickly resuming his woebegone expression*)   Just
complaining about how poor I am. Here I am with a
grown daughter who hasn't a dime to her dowry and can
never get married. Who could I possibly marry her off to?

MEGADORUS (*clapping him on the back*)   Don't say such
things! Cheer up, Euclio! There'll be a dowry; I'll help you
out. Whatever you need, just say the word. Give me your
orders.

EUCLIO (*to the audience, with a crafty look*)   Promising to
give—which means he's out to get; he's got his mouth
agape to gulp my gold. While one hand holds out a piece
of bread, the other hides a stick. Any rich man who's so

nice and generous to somebody poor, I just don't trust. He puts out a helping hand—and it leaves a trail of damage. I know these octopuses. Whatever they touch, they take.

MEGADORUS (*gravely*)   Euclio, give me a minute of your time. There's something I'd like to discuss with you—won't take long—which should be a good thing for both of us.

EUCLIO (*to the audience, frantically*)   Oh my god, I'm done for! My gold's been snitched! And now he wants to make a deal with me, I know it! I've got to take a look in the house. (*Whirls about and heads for his door.*)

MEGADORUS (*calling after him in surprise*)   Where are you going?

EUCLIO (*over his shoulder*)   Be right back—something I've got to see in the house. (*He disappears inside.*)

MEGADORUS (*to himself, worriedly*)   Damn, I'm afraid that the minute I mention marrying his daughter, he'll think I'm playing a joke on him. Poverty's made him the stingiest man alive, bar none.

(*The door opens, and Euclio emerges in a considerably better frame of mind than he had been in a moment before.*)

EUCLIO (*to the audience*)   The good lord's watching over me: it's safe. By safe I only mean it isn't gone. (*Shaking his head*) That was a bad scare I had. I almost died before I got back in the house. (*To Megadorus*) Back again, Megadorus. Now, do you want me for anything?

MEGADORUS   Thank you. (*Gravely*) I hope you don't mind answering some questions I'd like to ask you.

EUCLIO (*darting a sharp glance at him*)   No—providing you don't ask anything I mind answering.

MEGADORUS   Tell me, what's your opinion of my family background?

EUCLIO   Good.

MEGADORUS   Of my integrity?

EUCLIO   Good.

MEGADORUS   My conduct?

EUCLIO   Not bad. Not dishonest.

MEGADORUS   And you know how old I am.

EUCLIO   Yes. *And* how rich.

MEGADORUS (*enthusiastically*)   Now, I consider you a fine, upstanding member of the community, and always have.

EUCLIO (*to the audience, in consternation*)   He's sniffed my gold! (*To Megadorus, coldly*) Just what is it you want from me?

MEGADORUS   You know the kind of man I am, and I know the kind you are. With that clear, I'm asking you for the hand of your daughter—and, god willing, it will mean happiness for me, you, and her. (*Earnestly*) Promise me you'll do it!

EUCLIO (*bitingly*)   Look here, Megadorus. This conduct does no credit to the way you've conducted yourself in the past. Making fun of a poor old man who's never done any harm to you or your family! I never did, I never said one thing to justify doing to me what you're doing to me now.

MEGADORUS (*helplessly*)   Good god! I'm not here to make fun of you, and I'm *not* making fun of you. I wouldn't think of such a thing!

EUCLIO (*suspiciously*)   Then why are you asking to marry my daughter?

MEGADORUS (*earnestly*)   So you can be better off because of me, and I because of you and your daughter.

EUCLIO (*coldly*)   Here's something that occurs to me, Megadorus. You're a rich man, one of the upper crust, and I'm poor, poor as they come. Suppose I let you marry my daughter. It occurs to me that we'd be like a bull and a donkey and, when donkey Euclio is hitched up with bull Megadorus and can't pull his share of the load, donkey Euclio is going to go down in the mud, and bull Megadorus is not going to bother looking back; he's going to act as if the donkey never was. I'll find out that you're not going to treat me as an equal, while my own class is going to laugh at me. And, should there be a divorce, things really will be unstable—I won't have a stable in either camp: the donkeys are going to maul me with their teeth and the bulls gore me with their horns. It's a risky business, this moving up from the donkeys to the bulls.

MEGADORUS (*earnestly*)   Why, the very best thing you could possibly do is be connected with, and as closely as you can, the right kind of people. Listen to me—accept my offer, let me have her.

EUCLIO (*hastily*)   But I can't give you a dowry.

MEGADORUS   Don't! Let her come with a fine character, and she'll have dowry enough.

EUCLIO   I just brought it up so you wouldn't get the idea (*forcing a laugh*) I suddenly found a buried treasure.

MEGADORUS (*smiling*)   I know, you don't have to tell me. Just say yes.

EUCLIO   Yes. (*Suddenly hearing a clink*) Oh my god in heaven, is this to be the end of me?

MEGADORUS (*puzzled*)   What's the matter with you?

EUCLIO   Wasn't there a sound like a shovel just then? (*Whirls about and dashes into his house.*)

MEGADORUS (*turning to point toward his own house*)   It's from my garden. I gave orders to do some digging there. (*Turning back and seeing no Euclio, to himself*) Hey, where *is* the man? Off he goes without letting me know where I stand! (*Sadly*) He sees I want to be his friend, so he turns up his nose at me. He's doing just what they all do. When somebody rich tries to make friends with somebody poor, the poor man's always afraid to get involved. And his fears make him lose out because, invariably, after he's passed up the chance and it's too late, he gets second thoughts.

(*The door opens, and Euclio comes out again. He turns to talk to Grape inside.*)

EUCLIO (*through the doorway, snarling*)   So help me, if I

don't have that tongue of yours torn out by the roots, I hereby give you full permission to arrange with anyone you want to have me castrated! (*Turns and walks back to Megadorus.*)

MEGADORUS (*angrily*)   It's damned clear to me that, in spite of my gray hairs, and for no good reason at all, you consider me an ideal subject to play games with.

EUCLIO (*hastily*)   Believe me, Megadorus, I'm not playing games. (*Aside, bitterly*) Not much chance, even if I wanted to!

MEGADORUS (*impatiently*)   Well, what do you say? Do I get to marry your daughter?

EUCLIO   With the understanding she gets the amount of dowry I mentioned.

MEGADORUS (*nodding vigorous assent*)   Then you're giving me your solemn word?

EUCLIO   I'm giving you my solemn word.

MEGADORUS (*beaming*)   God bless us all!

EUCLIO   Amen. (*Sharply*) Be sure you don't forget our agreement: you don't get a penny of dowry with my daughter.

MEGADORUS   I haven't forgotten.

EUCLIO (*sneering*)   I'm wise to the way you and your kind can mix a man up: it's on, it's off; it's off, it's on—just the way *you* want it.

MEGADORUS (*firmly*)   You'll have no cause to get into any arguments with me. Now, about the wedding. Is there any reason why we shouldn't hold it today?

EUCLIO   None at all. That would be perfect.

MEGADORUS (*promptly*)   Then I'll go and get things ready. Don't need me for anything, do you?

EUCLIO (*promptly*)   Nothing except what you're doing. Run along. Good-by.

MEGADORUS (*rushing to the door of his house and calling*

through the doorway)   Hey, Strobilus! Hurry and follow
me to the market. On the double!

*(A slave comes dashing out of the house, and the two race
off, stage left.)*

EUCLIO *(to the audience)*   There he goes. Lord in heaven!
I tell you, money sure is strong stuff! I'm convinced he's
heard I have a fortune in the house and is drooling at the
mouth to get at it. That's why he's so set on joining the
family. *(Walking to his door and calling through the doorway)* Where's the old hag who's been babbling to all the
neighbors that I'm going to give my daughter a dowry?
(Roaring) Grape! I'm calling you! Are you deaf? *(As she
appears at the doorway)* Hurry and wash that handful of
dishware we have. I've arranged for my daughter's marriage. I promised her to Megadorus, and the wedding's to
be today.

GRAPE   God bless them both! *(Suddenly dismayed)* But it
can't be today! That's too soon!

EUCLIO   Shut up and go inside. Make sure everything's taken
care of by the time I get back from downtown. And keep
the door shut! I'll be back soon. *(Rushes off, stage left.)*

GRAPE *(to the audience, in consternation)*   Now what do I
do? This is the end of both of us, me *and* the young mistress! It won't be long before the whole world knows that
his daughter's disgraced, that she's going to have a baby.
We kept it a deep, dark secret up to now, but we can't any
longer. I'll go in now so I'll have all his orders done by the
time he gets back. *(Shaking her head ruefully)* I'm scared
to death I'll be drinking a double dose of trouble—whip
and woe in one!

*(Grape goes into the house. A moment later there enters,
stage left, a good-sized retinue: at the head is Megadorus'
servant Strobilus, "twister," followed by two cooks, Charcoal
[Anthrax] and Eel [Congrio, from conger, "conger eel"],
two pipers, and a flock of scullions loaded down with food
for the wedding banquet.)*

STROBILUS (*to the assemblage*)   After my master finished with the shopping and with hiring you cooks and pipers downtown, his orders to me were to divide everything he had gotten into two.

CHARCOAL   Damn it all, you're not going (*making an obscene gesture*) to split me, I tell you that right now. If you want all of me to go somewhere, all right.

EEL (*caustically*)   So demure and bashful, this little whore! All anyone has to do is ask you; you're always ready and willing (*repeating the gesture*) to do a split.

STROBILUS (*to Charcoal*)   I didn't mean what you're insinuating, Charcoal. The master's having a wedding today—

CHARCOAL (*interrupting*)   Whose daughter is he marrying?

STROBILUS (*gesturing toward Euclio's house*)   Our next door neighbor, Euclio's. And Euclio's to get half of what was bought, plus one of you cooks and one of the pipers. Master's orders.

CHARCOAL   As I get it then, (*pointing to Euclio's house*) half to his house, (*pointing to Megadorus'*) and half to his.

STROBILUS   As I get it, you're absolutely right.

CHARCOAL (*gesturing toward Euclio's house*)   What's the matter? Can't the old man there pay for his daughter's wedding out of his own pocket?

STROBILUS (*snorting*)   Pah!

CHARCOAL   What's that mean?

STROBILUS   You have to ask? Flint is fluff compared with that old boy!

CHARCOAL   You don't say?

EEL   You mean that?

STROBILUS   Just imagine . . . [a line is lost here] . . . he thinks he's ruined, wiped out. If a puff of smoke comes out of that shack of his, the next minute he's hollering to high heaven. Do you know, when he goes to bed he ties a bag over his mouth!

CHARCOAL What for?

STROBILUS So he won't lose any breath while he sleeps.

CHARCOAL (*scornfully*) Sure, and I suppose he plugs up the pipe at his lower end so he won't lose any wind while he sleeps.

STROBILUS (*offended*) You believe me, and I'll believe you. That's what I believe is only fair.

CHARCOAL (*hastily*) Oh no, I believe you.

STROBILUS Do you know something else? After he washes, it breaks his heart to throw away the water.

CHARCOAL (*grinning*) You think we can talk the old boy out of fifteen thousand dollars to set us all free?

STROBILUS He wouldn't even stake you to the chance to starve if you asked him for it. Do you know, the other day when he had his nails manicured at the barber's, he collected all the clippings and took them home with him!

CHARCOAL (*wonderingly*) Boy, oh boy, this is one stingy man you're talking about!

STROBILUS Can you imagine a person being that miserly and living that miserably? The other day a buzzard made off with his helping of dinner. He bawled like a baby, went to the judge, and, crying his heart out, asked whether he couldn't have the bird subpoenaed. Oh, I could give you hundreds of stories, if I had the time. (*Getting down to business and looking from Charcoal to Eel*) Now, which of you two is faster? Tell me.

CHARCOAL (*promptly*) I am. (*Going through a practiced gesture of slipping something into his pocket*) And lots better, too.

STROBILUS (*eying him distastefully*) I'm talking about a cook, not a crook.

CHARCOAL (*innocently*) That's what I mean, a cook.

STROBILUS (*to Eel*) What about you?

EEL (*drawing himself up, importantly*) See for yourself.

CHARCOAL (*contemptuously*)   He's a Sunday cook—it's the only day of the week he gets work.

EEL (*to Charcoal*)   Look who's making nasty cracks about *me!* A man who needs only five letters to spell his name—C-R-O-O-K!

CHARCOAL   Aah, you're one yourself. A lousy crook!

STROBILUS (*shouting*)   Shut up! (*To Charcoal*) Now pick whichever of these two lambs is fatter and take it into my house.

CHARCOAL   All right.

STROBILUS (*to Eel*)   Eel, take the other one and (*pointing to Euclio's door*) go to that house. (*To one half of the assistants*) You follow him. (*To the others*) The rest of you over there to my house. (*Charcoal leads them into Megadorus' house.*)

EEL (*hollering*)   Hey, this division is unfair! Their lamb is fatter!

STROBILUS (*promptly*)   But you're getting a fatter piper. (*To one of the pipers*) Phrygia! (*Pointing to Eel*) Follow him. (*To the other*) Eleusium, you go over there into my house. (*Eleusium follows the others into Megadorus' house.*)

EEL (*angrily*)   Pretty canny, Strobilus—shoving me off over here with the old skinflint! If I need anything, I'll have to ask till I get hoarse before he'll give it to me.

STROBILUS (*contemptuously*)   Stupid! (*Shaking his head in exasperation*) What's the good of doing *you* a good turn? Just a waste of effort!

EEL (*weakly*)   A good turn? How?

STROBILUS   What a question! In the first place, in the house you're going to, there'll be no fuss and bother around you. Next, if you need anything, you won't waste your breath asking for it, you'll just go get it from home. Over here there's a big household and lots of fuss and bother. Plus furniture, silverware, money, clothes. Over here, if anything disappears—and remember, it's easy to keep hands off where there's nothing to put them on—the next minute they're all hollering (*mimicking*), "The cooks stole it! Arrest 'em, whip 'em, tie 'em up, throw 'em in jail!" None of this is going to happen to you because there's going to be nothing you can make off with. This way. Follow me.

EEL   Coming.

(*Strobilus, followed by Eel and the rest of the retinue, walks up to Euclio's door and knocks.*)

STROBILUS (*shouting*)   Hey, Grape! Come to the door and open up!

GRAPE (*from inside*)   Who is it?

STROBILUS (*shouting*)   Strobilus.

GRAPE (*opening the door*)   What do you want?

STROBILUS   Take these cooks, this piper, and this stuff we bought for the wedding banquet. Megadorus left orders to deliver it all to Euclio.

GRAPE (*eying the bundles; sourly*)   You planning to hold a wedding for a water nymph?

STROBILUS   Why?

GRAPE   I see you haven't brought a drop to drink.

STROBILUS (*reassuringly*)   It's coming later, when Megadorus gets back from downtown.

GRAPE (*to Eel, sourly*)   We don't have any firewood.

EEL   You have rafters, don't you?

GRAPE   Of course we have rafters.

EEL   Then we have firewood. Don't bother going out to look.

GRAPE (*shrieking*)   You filthy good-for-nothing! *You* may be a fire worshiper, but don't ask *us* to burn our house down just to let you cook a dinner and collect a salary!

EEL (*backing down*)   I'm not asking you to.

STROBILUS   Take them all inside.

GRAPE   Follow me.

(*Eel and his party follow Grape into Euclio's house while Strobilus goes into Megadorus' house.*

A moment later, one of Megadorus' household slaves comes out of the door. He turns and talks to the others inside. [This servant, named Pythodicus in the manuscripts, does not re-appear. Very likely his whole speech was not written by Plautus but, after his death, was added by some actor or editor.])

SERVANT (*through the doorway*) Take care of it. I'll go see what the cooks are doing. (*Walking downstage and addressing the audience, grumbling*) That's my biggest headache today, keeping an eye on those cooks. The only other thing I could do is have them make dinner in a dungeon. When it was done we could haul it up in baskets. Then, if they eat up everything they cooked down there, (*grinning*) the lords of hell would be having a feast and those above a famine. But look at me standing around and talking as if I had nothing to do, when we've got all those damned sons of vultures in the house!

(*He turns and rushes back into Megadorus' house. A moment later Euclio stomps in, stage left.*)

EUCLIO (*to the audience*) In order to do the right thing by my daughter at her wedding, I was willing to take my life in my hands—I went to the market. I asked the price of fish. Dear. Lamb? Dear. Beef? Dear. Veal, tuna, pork? All of them dear. And my having no money made everything even dearer! I left the place hopping mad since I couldn't buy a thing—but I had my fun with that filthy pack of peddlers, I did!

On the way home I began to think things over: splurge on the holidays, I figure, and it's scrimp or go without on the weekdays. I announced this line of reasoning to my belly and heart, and my mind came around to my way of thinking: to marry off my daughter at minimum expense. (*Holding out a tiny packet and some sad-looking garlands*) So I bought this pinch of incense and these garlands; I'll put them in the fireplace for the Spirit of the House and get his blessing on my daughter's union. (*Turning to go into the house*) What's this I see? The door open? And listen to the racket coming from inside! Oh, my god, is this a robbery?

EEL (*from inside*) Go next door and ask if they've got a bigger pot. This one's small, it doesn't hold enough.

EUCLIO (*to the audience, agonized*) God in heaven, I'm done for! They're making off with my gold, and they need a bigger pot! (*Raising his eyes to heaven, fervently*) Apollo! I beg you, save me! Help! If you've ever come to the rescue at a time like this, do it now! Shoot your arrows at these crooks—they're treasury thieves![2] (*Clapping a hand to his brow*) What am I waiting here for? Why don't I run in before I'm completely ruined!

(*Euclio charges into his house. A moment later Charcoal emerges from Megadorus' house. He turns to speak to his assistants inside.*)

CHARCOAL (*through the doorway*) Sprinter, clean the fish. Cutter, fillet the eels, and make it snappy! I'm going next door to borrow a baking pan from Eel. And, if you're smart, you'll have that chicken plucked smoother than a ballet dancer. (*Starts to go toward Euclio's house when a hullabaloo is suddenly heard coming from it. To himself*) What's all the noise next door? (*Shrugging*) Must be the cooks carrying on the vocal part of their job. I'll run back inside to make sure *we* don't have a ruckus like that.

(*Charcoal goes back into Megadorus' house, and the stage is now empty.*)

[2] Apollo would theoretically have a fellow sufferer's sympathy: his temples were used as treasuries and were often the targets of plunderers and thieves.

ACT III

(*The din in Euclio's house grows louder and louder. Suddenly the door flies open and Eel, clutching his carving knife, bursts out, followed by his crew, all traveling at top speed.*)

SONG

EEL (*to the world at large*)

Hey, citizens, aliens, women, children, men, hey all of you!
Get off the streets and leave them clear—make way, I'm coming through!
First time I've worked as madhouse cook, and catered to lunatics!
My god, the way they went for us, and beat us up with sticks!
The old boy made me his punching bag, I ache all over, I'm dead.
No wood? There's more in there than any place else, the supply's unlimited!
He laid on us all the wood he could before he sent us out!

(*The door opens, and Euclio appears brandishing a stick.*)

My god, I'm lost! The door's just opened—that lunatic's about!

(*As Euclio spots him and charges*)

He's after me! But I've worked out just what I have to do—
He's taught me the lesson himself, he has: he's running, so I run too!

(*The two race around the stage at top speed.*)

EUCLIO (*screaming*)

Come back! Hey, where are you running? Stop him!

EEL

                             Dumbbell! Why this shouting?

(*They come to a halt and glare at each other.*)

EUCLIO (*grimly*)

I'm going to give the police your name.

EEL

                    And why?

EUCLIO (*pointing*)

                              That knife you're flouting.

EEL (*helplessly*)

But I'm a cook!

EUCLIO (*darkly*)

              You threatened me—now tell me why you did it.

EEL (*eying his knife and shaking his head regretfully*)

I'm afraid I goofed. Between your ribs is where I should
have hid it.

EUCLIO (*snarling*)

You're a dirty crook, that's what you are, beyond all human
measure.

There's no one I'd rather do more harm, or do it with
greater pleasure.

EEL (*ruefully*)

No need to tell me, the case is clear—just witness my condition.

With my broken bones, a contortionist couldn't give me
competition.

(*Drawing himself up*)

How dare a beggar like you touch me?

EUCLIO (*sneering*)

                              He asks how dare I do it!

(*Brandishing the stick*)

Perhaps you mean I stopped too soon, and you want me to
pursue it?

EEL (*brandishing the knife*)

Lay off, or, I swear, you'll pay for it, while I'm alive and
kicking.

EUCLIO (*caressing his club and grinning malevolently*)

The future I'll not answer for, but right now you sure are
kicking!

(*Sternly*)

While I was away you entered my house without asking
    my permission.

What *were* you doing? I want to know!

EEL (*wearily*)

                            You can stop the inquisition.

We came to cook for the wedding feast.

EUCLIO (*sneering*)

                        What the hell do *you* care, mister,

If the food I eat is raw or cooked? Since when are you big
    sister?

EEL (*as before*)

I want an answer, yes or no: will you let us do our cooking?

EUCLIO

I want an answer: about my things—will they be safe? No
    crooking?

EEL (*fervently*)

Just let me get home with the things I brought. I like
    them, yours don't attract me.

EUCLIO (*with ponderous irony*)

Oh sure. I know. Don't mention it.

EEL (*puzzled*)

                  What's the reason you attacked me

So we couldn't cook the dinner inside? Was it something we
    did or said there

That wasn't exactly what you wished?

EUCLIO (*exploding*)

             You ask, after poking that head there

Into every corner of my house. Your job was by the fire.

You weren't there, so I split your skull; you deserve what
    you got, you liar!

And now's the time to make things clear, so you know
    what's my position:

You take a single step toward this door without express
    permission,

And I make you the saddest man alive. So now you know
   my feeling.

(*Euclio about-faces and starts stalking off toward his
house.*)

EEL (*calling after him, agonized*)
   Hey, where are you going? Come back! COME BACK! I
      swear, by our Lady of Stealing,
   You hand me back my pots and pans, or a spectacle com-
      mences:
   I stand out here and howl and yowl till I drive you out of
      your senses.

(*Euclio storms into the house and slams the door.*)

   Now what? My god, what lousy luck that I ever went
      through that door—
   My pay for today is just five dollars; my doctor bills will be
      more!

(*A moment later the door opens again, and Euclio comes
out. His arm is pressed to his side to hold a pot hidden under
his coat.*)

EUCLIO (*to the audience*)   So help me, from now on this
   stays with me, I take it wherever I go. I'm not leaving it
   in such mortal danger ever again! (*To Eel and his party*)
   Hey, cooks, pipers, all of you! You can go in now. (*To
   Eel*) Take that gang of slaveys in now, if you want. Go
   ahead—cook, work, run around. Anything you want.

EEL (*glaring at him*)   Fine time to tell me—after splitting
   my skull with that stick!

EUCLIO   Go on in. You were hired for cooking, not looking.

EEL   Listen you, I'm damned well going to collect damages
   from you for this beating. I was hired as a cook, not a
   punching bag.

EUCLIO (*shrugging*)   Go ahead, sue me—but don't bother

me now! Come on, either get that dinner cooked or get away from this house—and go straight to hell.

EEL (*aside, growling*)   Aah, go there yourself. (*He leads his party back into the house.*)

EUCLIO (*watching the last one go in and then turning to the audience*)   He's left. (*Bitterly*) You need a lot of nerve if you're a poor man and you let yourself get involved with the rich. Look what Megadorus is doing. He's going after me in every way he can. He makes believe that he's sending cooks here to show how much he thinks of me, but you know what the real reason is? So they can sneak (*patting the pot*) this away from me! (*With even more bitterness*) My rooster was just as bad; he used to belong to the old hag, and he came damned near destroying me. He began scratching all around where this was buried. Well, it just made my blood boil. So I grabbed a club and brained him. Dirty thief caught in the act! Damn it, if you ask me, those crooks bribed that rooster to reveal where this was. (*Grinning*) The snatchers lost their scratcher—and I was in a cockfight! (*His attention caught, suddenly looks toward the wings, stage left.*) Look who's coming—my in-law Megadorus, back from downtown. I don't dare go by him any longer without stopping and passing the time of day.

(*Enter Megadorus deep in thought. Without noticing Euclio, he makes his way downstage and addresses the audience.*)

MEGADORUS   I told a lot of my friends about my plans and this arrangement I've made. They approved of Euclio's daughter and said I was making a smart and sensible move.

(*Earnestly*) In my opinion, others should do the same thing. If the men who have the money were to go to those who don't, ask for their daughters without dowries, and marry them, there'd be a lot more good feeling in our city. We'd have less envy than we have now, our wives would show us more respect than we're getting now, and we'd

spend lots less than we do now. For most of the people it
would be the best thing in the world. We'd have a fight
on our hands with only a few selfish ones, people who are
so grasping and greedy neither the law nor the lash can
control them.

(*After a moment's thought*) I suppose someone will
want to know who the rich girls with dowries are going to
marry if we pass such a law favoring the poor. Well, let
them marry whoever they like—providing no dowry goes
with them. Under my system, they'll develop some decent
traits and bring these as dowry instead of what they bring
now. (*Pounding his fist into the palm of his hand*) Why,
my system would drop the price of fancy carriage mules—
which today cost you more than a horse—below the price
of ordinary nags!

EUCLIO (*aside, rapturously*)   Believe me, it's a sheer pleasure to listen to him. Marvelous plea for parsimony he's
made.

MEGADORUS   And then none of our wives will be able to say,
(*mimicking a nagging female*) "The dowry I brought you
was far more than all the money you had in the world. So
I have every right to silks and jewelry and maids and
coach mules and coachmen and footmen and errand boys
and my own carriages."

EUCLIO (*aside, approvingly*)   This man really knows the
way our fancy ladies carry on. I'd like to see him appointed
Commissioner of Women's Ways.

MEGADORUS (*bitterly*)   Nowadays, whatever house in town
you go to, you see more vehicles standing around than
when you go to a country farm. But these are practically
a pleasure compared with the crowds standing around who
are after your money. There's the cleaner, the embroiderer,
the jeweler, the clothier. Then the salesmen—lace, lingerie,
red-dye, violet-dye, yellow-dye, coats, perfume. Add the
chemisiers, the shoemakers, the slipper makers, the sandal
makers. Plus the dyers. Plus the launderers. Plus the seam-

stresses. Plus the brassiere makers and corset makers. (*Shakes his head in despair.*)

When you think you finally have them all paid off, in troop another three hundred to start dunning, and your foyer is filled with bagmakers, weavers, fancy-dress makers, cabinetmakers. They're ushered in, they get their money, you think once and for all you have the whole pack paid, and in troop the dyers (yellow-dyers this time)—(*throwing up his hands*) there's always some damned pain-in-the-neck around trying to get something out of you!

EUCLIO (*aside*) I'd go up and talk to him but I'm afraid he'll cut short these wonderful words on the ways of women. So I'll just let him be.

MEGADORUS Then, when you've finally settled accounts with all these rubbish peddlers, at the last minute in comes an old veteran of the wars. He asks for a loan. He steps outside while you check your account with your banker. He waits around, famished, thinking he's going to get his loan. You finish figuring your balance with your banker, and find *you* need a loan! So the soldier has to put off his hopes till some other time. (*Heaving a sigh*) These and plenty of others are the tribulations and expenses, enough to crush a man, that come with large dowries. Now, you take a girl *without* a dowry—a husband can lay down the law to her! But the ones with—(*shaking his head dolefully*) they can drive a poor husband to death with debt and drudgery. (*Turns and catches sight of Euclio.*) Ah, there's my in-law in front of his house. Hello there, Euclio.

EUCLIO (*beaming*) I enjoyed your talk no end. Just ate it up.

MEGADORUS (*surprised*) You heard what I said?

EUCLIO Every word, right from the beginning.

MEGADORUS (*eying Euclio's get-up unhappily*) All the same, I don't think it would be a bad idea if you'd spruce up a bit for your daughter's wedding.

EUCLIO (*putting on his woebegone look*)   Family pride is only for people with the money to dress and the means for display. Believe me, Megadorus, I and every other poor man, we're every bit as bad off as people think.

MEGADORUS (*benignly*)   No, no. You have all you need, and may the good lord keep it that way. May he guard and increase what you have now!

EUCLIO (*abruptly turning away to address the audience, nervously*)   "What you have now"—I don't like that kind of talk! (*Patting the pot*) He knows as well as I do that I have this. The old hag told him everything!

MEGADORUS (*jovially*)   What's this? Leaving the floor of the senate for a private confabulation?

EUCLIO (*turning back, in a blind fury*)   God damn it, I was getting ready to accuse you to your face the way you deserve!

MEGADORUS (*astonished*)   What's the matter?

EUCLIO (*as before*)   You have to ask? After filling my house, every corner in it, full of thieves? After sending into my house five hundred cooks? A bunch of Geryons they were, each one with six hands! Argus himself couldn't keep an eye on them, that fellow who was nothing but eyes, the one who guarded Io for Juno.[3] Then that piper! If Fount Pirene at Corinth would only gush wine, she could drink it dry all by herself! And the stuff you bought—

MEGADORUS (*helplessly*)   My god, it was enough for an army! I even sent a lamb over—

EUCLIO (*witheringly*)   I don't know of any animal anywhere more devout than that lamb.

---

[3] One of Hercules' labors involved fighting a monster called Geryon who, being triple-bodied, had six arms, six legs, and so on.

Io, one of Jupiter's inamoratas, was turned into a heifer, and Juno set Argus, who had eyes all over his head and body, to guarding her.

MEGADORUS (*bewildered*)   Would you mind telling me just how that lamb is devout?

EUCLIO (*promptly*)   Look at all the fasting he's done—he's emaciated, nothing but skin and bones. Hold him up to the light, and you can inspect his entrails while he's still alive. He's like a lantern, he's transparent.

MEGADORUS (*as before*)   I paid for having him slaughtered!

EUCLIO   Then the best thing for you to do is pay for having him buried instead. Because, if you ask me, by now he's passed away.

MEGADORUS (*deciding to overlook all this as harmless eccentricity, heartily*)   Euclio, I want you to have a drink with me today.

EUCLIO (*snarling*)   I'm not doing any damned drinking!

MEGADORUS (*dismayed*)   But I'm having a whole cask of vintage wine delivered to the house!

EUCLIO   None for me. Made a resolution to drink only water.

MEGADORUS (*clapping him on the back*)   Well, water-drinker, sure as I'm alive, I'll have you soused before the day is over!

EUCLIO (*to the audience, looking crafty*)   I know what he's out to do! Get me dead drunk, that's the tack he's taking. Then, afterwards, this pot I have here will have a change of address. But I'll fix that—I'll hide this somewhere outside the house. Make it all a waste of his wine and time, that's what I'll do.

MEGADORUS (*turning to go*)   Well, unless you need me for something, I'll be off. Got to wash up for the ceremony. (*He enters his house.*)

EUCLIO (*holding up his pot*)   God in heaven, pot, you and this money you're taking care of have a lot of enemies! The best thing to do now is to take you into the Temple of Trust. I can find a good hiding place for you in there. (*Walking up to the door of the temple*) My Lady of Trust, you know me and I know you. Just watch out that you don't change your name if I trust (*slapping the pot*) this to you. I trust you'll be trustworthy, Trust; that's why I'm here.

(*He enters the temple, and the stage is now empty.*)

ACT IV

(*Enter, stage left, Lyconides' servant, Strobilus, a smug, swaggering type who, it is immediately apparent, has plenty of time to look after his own interests and is well able to do so.* [Why he has the same name as Megadorus' servant is hard to explain; it may be the result of ancient tampering with the text.])

STROBILUS (*to the audience*)   What I'm doing now is what all good servants should do: not regard the master's orders as a nuisance and waste of time. A servant who's out to serve the way his master wants him to, should serve the master first and fast, and himself second. If he takes time out to sleep, let him remember in his sleep that he's on call.

(*Pauses to let this sink in, then continues.*) Now, if a servant serves a master who's in love, which is my situation, I consider it said servant's sworn duty, when he sees love getting the upper hand, to save him by holding him back, and never to egg him on in the direction he's heading. It's like boys learning to swim: they're given little reed rafts to help them save their strength and make it easier for them to move their arms and swim; well, my theory is that, when a master's in love, his servant should be his raft, should keep him up and not let him sink to the bottom like a lump of lead.

(*Warming up to his theme*) He should know what the master wants just by reading the look on his face. He should race to carry out orders faster than any race horse. If he does all this, he'll avoid rawhide expressions of disapproval, and he'll never put a shine on a set of shackles with his shins.

(*Stops for a moment, and then continues confidentially.*) Now, my master's in love with the daughter (*gesturing toward Euclio's house*) of this pauper Euclio here. The boy's just gotten word that the girl's engaged to marry (*gesturing toward Megadorus' house*) Megadorus here. So he's sent me to scout the situation and get a line on what's going on. (*Eying the altar in front of the Temple of Trust*) I can take a seat on this altar right here, and no one will suspect a thing. And from here, I can keep an eye on what's doing (*pointing to Euclio's house*) here and (*pointing to Megadorus' house*) here.

(*He sits down. A second later Euclio emerges from the temple. Without noticing that he is being overheard, he turns and addresses the Goddess of Trust.*)

EUCLIO   Lady Trust, take care you don't let a soul know that my money's in there. I'm not afraid of anyone finding it by himself: it's in a good dark corner. (*Waggling a warning finger*) The man who uncovers that potful of gold will make himself a pretty penny, believe you me, so I beg of you, Lady Trust, don't let it happen! I'm going off now to wash. I want to be ready for the ceremony and not hold up my son-in-law: let him take the girl off to his house the minute he comes for her. Look sharp, Lady Trust, and I mean SHARP! I want to be sure to get my pot back from you safe and sound. I'm trusting the money to you—it's in the temple inside your shrine. (*Exits, stage left.*)

STROBILUS   (*springing from his seat and running downstage to address the audience*)   God in heaven! What I just heard that man say! That he hid a whole potful of gold here in the Temple of Trust! (*Turning and addressing the temple*) Please, goddess, don't show *him* more trust than me! (*To the audience*) I think the girl my master's in love with is this man's daughter. Well, while he's busy somewhere else, I'll go in and have a look around the temple to see if I can find the money. (*To the temple*) And, if I do, my lady, I'll ladle you out one full gallon of the best sacramental wine. That's what I'll do for you. (*To the audience, confidentially*) And after I've done it, I'll do something for myself by guzzling it all.

(*Strobilus races into the temple. The next moment Euclio comes rushing back, stage left.*)

EUCLIO (*To the audience, nervously*)   There must be a good
reason why a black cat crossed my path just now, and from
the left, no less! And all the time, it kept scratching the
ground with its claws and yowling and yowling. My heart
started right in doing a jig and jumping up into my throat.
But why stand here? I've got to run!

(*He races into the temple. Sounds of a scuffle, then, a moment later, out he comes, hauling Strobilus by the ear.*)

EUCLIO (*raging and punching away*)   Outside, you! You
must have crawled in there underground, you worm! A
minute ago you were nowhere to be seen, and, now that
you've appeared, you're going to disappear! God damn it,
you'll get it from me, you dirty thief!

STROBILUS (*blustering, as he tries to dodge the shower of
blows*)   What the hell's got into you? I've got nothing to
do with you, you old goat! What are you hitting me for?
What are you hauling me off for? What do you mean by
beating me up this way?

EUCLIO (*snarling*)   A born beatable, and he has to ask!
You're three times as crooked as any crook, you crook!

STROBILUS (*switching from bluster to high dudgeon*)   What
did I ever steal from you?

EUCLIO (*grimly*)   Give it back.

STROBILUS   What do you want me to give back?

EUCLIO   What a question!

STROBILUS (*switching to incredulity*)   You *robbed?* By *me?*

EUCLIO (*snarling*)   *You* robbed. *From* me. Hand it over.
(*Getting no response*) Well, what about it?

STROBILUS   What about what?

EUCLIO   You won't get away with it.

STROBILUS   What are you after, anyway?

EUCLIO (*menacingly*)   Give it to me!

STROBILUS   Why, you old goat, you're the one who's always
(*with an obscene gesture*) giving it.

EUCLIO   Give it to me, I say! And cut out the jokes. I'm not fooling now.

STROBILUS *(resentfully)*   What do you want me to give? Why don't you tell me what it is? Believe me, I never in all my life put a hand on anything of yours. Not even a finger!

EUCLIO   Hold out your hands.

STROBILUS *(promptly doing so)*   I've got 'em out. See?

EUCLIO *(snarling)*   Yes, I see. *(Baffled)* Better show me that third one you have.

STROBILUS *(to the world at large)*   This old boy is mad. He's crazy. He's seeing things. *(To Euclio, self-righteously indignant)* You think you're doing the right thing by me?

EUCLIO   Absolutely the wrong thing, I admit it. Hanging's the only right thing, and I'll do it, too, if you don't confess!

STROBILUS *(as if driven to desperation)*   Confess what!

EUCLIO *(glaring at him and pointing to the temple)*   What did you steal from there?

STROBILUS *(hand on heart)*   The good lord strike me dead on the spot if I stole anything of yours—*(aside)* also if I don't!

EUCLIO   Come on, shake out your coat.

STROBILUS *(promptly doing so, cheerfully)*   Anything you say.

EUCLIO *(biting his lip)*   Must be under your shirt.

STROBILUS *(cheerfully)*   Look wherever you like.

EUCLIO   You dirty rat! Being nice just to make me think you didn't steal it! I'm onto your tricks. *(Frisks him, finds nothing, and glares at him. Then, bitterly)* All right, hold out your right hand again.

STROBILUS *(as before)*   Here you are.

EUCLIO   Now the left one.

STROBILUS *(holding out both)*   Look, I'll hold out both at the same time.

EUCLIO *(bitterly)*   All right, no more searching. Just hand it over.

STROBILUS Hand over what?

EUCLIO (*witheringly*) Very funny. (*Snarling*) But I know you've got it!

STROBILUS (*shouting*) Got it? Got *what!*

EUCLIO (*looking crafty*) I won't tell you. You're too anxious to find out. (*Shouting*) Whatever you've got of mine, you hand over!

STROBILUS (*switching to exasperation*) You're out of your mind! You searched me all you wanted, and you didn't find a thing of yours on me. (*Turns and makes as if to walk away.*)

EUCLIO (*suddenly struck by a thought, grabbing him*) Stop, you! (*Pointing to the temple*) Who's in there? Who's the other fellow who was in there with you? (*To the world at large*) Oh my god, I'm a goner! There's another one making trouble in there right now—and if I let go, this one'll run away! (*Suddenly frowning in thought*) But, after all, I just searched him, he hasn't got anything. (*Letting go of him*) All right, you can go.

STROBILUS (*putting a safe distance between him and Euclio*) God damn you to hell and gone!

EUCLIO (*to the audience*) Fine thanks I get! (*To Strobilus, grimly*) Now I'll go in and get that accomplice of yours by the throat and strangle him. Are you going to get out of my sight or not?

STROBILUS (*taking a jump toward the wings, stage left*) I'm going.

EUCLIO Don't let me lay eyes on you again! (*Dashes into the temple.*)

STROBILUS (*to the audience, grimly*) I'd sooner die a slow death than not trap this old boy today! (*Thoughtfully*) He won't dare hide the money here any longer. My guess is he's going to bring it out right now and hide it someplace else. (*Turning to look as he hears the creaking of the door*) Ah—the door! And there's the old boy bringing

out his money. I'll just slip back here to this doorway for a
little while.

(*He takes his stand in an unobtrusive spot alongside the
door of Megadorus' house. A moment later Euclio emerges
from the temple with the pot under his coat.*)

EUCLIO (*not noticing Strobilus, to the audience*)   And I
thought Lady Trust could be trusted to a T! She came
damned near making a monkey out of me! If that cat
hadn't come to the rescue, I'd be a dead duck now. I only
wish the cat who tipped me off would come along so I
could do something nice for it—like saying a few nice words.
(*Sternly*) After all, throwing it something to eat would be
throwing food away.

(*Meditatively*) Now let me think of a secluded spot to
hide this. There's that grove of Lord Sylvanus[4] beyond
the city limits; it's all by itself in the middle of a mass of
willows. I'll pick a place there. (*Shaking his head ruefully*)
Believe me, I'd rather trust Lord Sylvanus than Lady Trust!
(*Rushes off, stage right.*)

STROBILUS (*to the audience, jubilantly*)   Well, well! Lady
Luck's taking care of me today! Now I'll just run ahead,
climb a tree in the forest, and watch from up there where
the old man hides the money. My orders are to stay right
here, but my mind's made up: I'll go looking for trouble—
when it pays off! (*Rushes off after Euclio.*)

(*Enter, stage left, Eunomia and her son, Lyconides, "wolf-
son." Lyconides is a good-looking young man in his early
twenties, expensively dressed, almost to the point of foppish-
ness. Normally he is as satisfied with himself and life as any
spoiled only son of an indulgent mother, but at this moment
he shows signs of considerable agitation.*)

LYCONIDES (*agitatedly*)   There, I've told you. Now you know
everything I do about what happened to Euclio's daugh-

[4] Sylvanus was god of the fields and forests.

ter. Mother, I begged you before and now I beg you again, Mother dear, please, PLEASE talk to Uncle!

EUNOMIA   You know very well that I want to see happen exactly what you do. And I'm sure I can get my brother to say yes to this. If it's all as you say it is, that you got drunk and violated the girl, then you've got every right to ask.

LYCONIDES   (*reproachfully*)   Mother dear! Would I lie to you? Right to your face?

(*A shriek is suddenly heard from inside Euclio's house.*)

PHAEDRIA   (*from inside*)   Oh, I'm dying! Nurse dear! Please! Oh, the pain! Oh god, help!

LYCONIDES   (*agonized*)   There you are, Mother! The facts speak louder than any words. She's screaming! She's giving birth right now!

EUNOMIA   (*resolutely, walking quickly toward the door of Megadorus' house*)   Come right inside with me to my brother. I'll get him to agree to what you want.

LYCONIDES   You go ahead, Mother. I'll follow in a second. (*To himself, menacingly*) I wonder where that servant of mine can be? I told him to meet me here! (*After a moment's thought*) But, on second thought, if he's off looking after my interests, it's wrong for me to blow up at him. (*Heaving a sigh*) I'll go in and join the jury that's judging my fàte.

(*He enters the house. A moment later Strobilus bounds in, stage right, clutching the pot.*)

STROBILUS   (*to the audience, ecstatically*)   Here's the one man in the world richer than the gnomes who live in the hills of gold! All your famous kings—I won't even bother mentioning them. (*Snapping his fingers*) Two-bit beggars! *I'm* Alexander the Great!

(*Shaking his head wonderingly*) What a day! After I left here a little while ago, I got there long before he came, and long before he came I was all set in a tree. From there I watched where the old man buried the money. When he left, I got down from my tree, dug up the potful of gold, and got out of there. I saw the old man on his way back, but he didn't see me; I kept a little off the road. (*His attention caught, looks toward the wings, stage right.*) Aha! There he is! Now I'll go and hide this in my house.)

(*Strobilus dashes off, stage left. A moment later Euclio staggers in, stumbling about blindly as if in a state of shock.*)

SONG

EUCLIO (*to the audience*)
>   I'm a goner! I'm finished! I'm through! I can't tell
>   Which direction to take and which not!

(*Shouting*)
>   Someone stop him!

(*Bewildered*)
>   But who? And stop who? I can't see,
>   I walk blindly, my brains are all shot!
>   Who knows where I am, who I am, where I'm going?

(*Addressing the spectators in the front row*)
>   You must help me, I implore you, you *must*.
>   Where's the robber who took it? Please show me, I beg
>   you!

(*To one of them*)
>   I say, mister, you're a man I can trust;
>   I can tell by your face that you're honest and good.

(*To the whole theater*)
>   What's the matter with you? What's so funny?

(*Bitterly*)
>   Oh I know what you're like, and I know in these seats
>   There are lots who know how to steal money.
>   With fine clothes and clean linen they sit there and look
>   Just like people who'd never stoop low.
>   No one here has my pot? Oh, you'll kill me, you will!

(*To a spectator in the first row*)

> Please tell me—who's got it? Don't know?

(*To the whole audience*)

> I'm destitute, derelict, done for, undone;
>> I'm down in the depths of despair.
> Oh the misery, mourning, and moans today's brought,
>> Plus starvation, the poorhouse, and care!
> I'm the deadest of mortals alive on this earth,
>> I've no need for my life any more.
> Oh the gold that I lost, which I'd guarded so well!
>> Oh the comforts and joys I forswore!
> And others will now have the pleasure and fun—
>> And who pays for it? I! I can't bear it!

LYCONIDES (*coming out of Megadorus' house*)

> Who's this weeping and wailing in front of our house?
>> Is it Euclio? Yes, I could swear it!
> Oh my god, I'm a goner! My secret is out!
>> He must know of his daughter's condition.
> Do I see him or flee him? Do I stay or go 'way?
>> Oh my god, what an awful position!

EUCLIO (*wheeling about*)   Who's talking there?

LYCONIDES (*coming forward to him*)   I. (*Heaving a sigh*) An unhappy man.

EUCLIO (*abjectly*)   No, I'm the unhappy man. Miserably unhappy. The trouble, the tragedy that's fallen on me!

LYCONIDES (*not very convincingly*)   Cheer up.

EUCLIO (*miserably*)   I ask you now, how can I possibly?

LYCONIDES (*hanging his head*)   Because the tragedy that's tormenting you was all my doing. I admit it.

EUCLIO (*unable to believe his ears*)   What did I hear you say?

LYCONIDES (*as before*)   The truth.

EUCLIO (*trembling with rage*)   Mister, what did I ever do to you that you should do this to me? Destroy me and my family this way?

LYCONIDES (*passionately*)   Some evil demon drove me to it, trapped me into doing it!

EUCLIO (*glaring at him*)   How?

LYCONIDES (*abjectly*)   I did wrong, I admit it. I deserve the blame, I know it. What's more, I'm here right now to beg you to be forbearing and forgive me.

EUCLIO (*wildly*)   How could you have had the gall to lay your hands on what wasn't yours to touch!

LYCONIDES (*dumbly*)   What do you want from me? What's done is done; it can't be undone. I think it was heaven's will. Otherwise it couldn't have happened, I know it.

EUCLIO (*snarling*)   And I think it's heaven's will that I take you into my house, throw you in chains, and murder you!

LYCONIDES (*shuddering*)   Don't say such things!

EUCLIO (*thundering*)   What do you mean by putting your hands on what's mine without my permission?

LYCONIDES (*barely audibly*)   It was wine and passion that drove me to do it.

EUCLIO (*as before*)   The colossal nerve of this man! How dare you come to me with that kind of talk? If the law gave the right to plead excuses like that, we could rob old ladies' purses on the street in broad daylight and, if caught, plead we did it because we were drunk and in love! Wine and passion are pretty poor things if they'll let any lush in love do what he likes and get away with it.

LYCONIDES (*humbly*)   I've come to you of my own free will to beg forgiveness for my stupidity.

EUCLIO (*sneering*)   I don't like people who do wrong and then excuse themselves. You know you had no right. You should have kept your hands off!

LYCONIDES   And just because I dared do what I shouldn't, I offer no excuses—(*rapturously*) let me keep this treasure, it's my dearest wish!

EUCLIO (*gasping*)   Keep my treasure? Against my will?

LYCONIDES (*hurriedly*)   Oh, I wouldn't ask to do it against

your will. But I do think it would be the right thing to do.
(*Earnestly*) I tell you, Euclio, even you'll come to see it's
the right thing to do.

EUCLIO (*staring at him uncomprehendingly, then exploding*)
God damn it, I'm going to haul you before the judge and
bring you up on charges unless you give me back—

LYCONIDES (*interrupting, bewildered*)   Give you back what?

EUCLIO   What you stole from me.

LYCONIDES (*as before*)   I stole something of yours? What?
From where?

EUCLIO (*sneering*)   Well, god bless you, you don't know!

LYCONIDES   Not unless you tell me what you're after.

EUCLIO (*grimly*)   I'll tell you. I'm asking you to hand back
the pot of gold you confessed you stole from me.

LYCONIDES (*taken aback*)   Good god in heaven! I never confessed or did any such thing!

EUCLIO   You deny it?

LYCONIDES   To my last breath I deny it! I don't know anything about any gold or what this pot of yours is.

EUCLIO   It's the one you stole from the grove of Sylvanus.
Come on, let's have it. (*In despair, starts wheedling*) Aw,
come on, give it back, won't you?

LYCONIDES (*incredulously*)   You must be crazy to call me a
thief, Euclio. I thought you had found out about something else, something that has to do with me. It's a very
important matter, and I'd like to talk it over with you
quietly, when you have a quiet moment.

EUCLIO (*looking at him piercingly*)   Tell me, on your word
of honor: you didn't steal the money?

LYCONIDES (*shaking his head vigorously*)   Word of honor.

EUCLIO   And you don't know who stole it?

LYCONIDES (*as before*)   Word of honor to that too.

EUCLIO   And if you find out who stole it, you'll tell me?

LYCONIDES (*nodding*)   Right.

EUCLIO   And you'll never go after a share of it or hide the thief?

LYCONIDES (*as before*)   Agreed.

EUCLIO   What if you go back on your word?

LYCONIDES (*raising his right hand and turning his eyes to heaven*)   Then may the good lord do with me what he wants.

EUCLIO   That's good enough for me. Now say whatever you want to.

LYCONIDES (*importantly*)   If you don't happen to know me or my family, (*gesturing toward Megadorus' house*) Megadorus here is my uncle, my father was Antimachus, my mother is Eunomia, and my name is Lyconides.

EUCLIO (*impatiently*)   The family I know. What I want to know is: what do you want now?

LYCONIDES (*as before*)   You have a daughter—

EUCLIO (*gesturing impatiently toward his house*)   Yes, right there in the house.

LYCONIDES   She's engaged, I believe, to marry my uncle?

EUCLIO (*wearily*)   You know all there is to know.

LYCONIDES   Well, my uncle has instructed me to tell you he's breaking the engagement.

EUCLIO (*unable to believe his ears*)   Breaking the engagement? Everything's arranged! Everything's ready for the wedding! (*Exploding*) I hope to god he fries in hell! It's because of him that I had the miserable luck to lose all that money today, god damn it!

LYCONIDES (*stoutly*)   Cheer up. And don't curse. May it all bring health and happiness to you and your daughter! (*Holding up his hand imperiously as Euclio opens his mouth*) Just say, "I pray to god it will."

EUCLIO (*fervently*)   I pray to god it will!

LYCONIDES   And I pray to god it will for my sake. Now listen. (*Earnestly*) Even the most worthless good-for-nothing, once he admits he's done wrong, is ashamed and wants to

clear himself. So now I implore you, Euclio, if I uninten-
tionally wronged you or your daughter, please forgive me
and let me marry her as the law requires. (*Hanging his
head*) You see, I have a confession to make: at the last
festival for Lady Ceres, I violated your daughter. I was
young and wild, and I had had too much to drink. . . .

EUCLIO (*clutching his head and shrieking*)   Ay-ay-ay! What
did I hear you say?

LYCONIDES (*deciding it was time to take the offensive, slapping him on the back*)   Why the ay-ay-ay's? You'll be a
grandfather when you go to your daughter's wedding,
thanks to me! She's having a baby! It's the ninth month;
figure it out. That's why my uncle broke off the engagement—it was for my sake. Go inside your house and ask.
Find out for yourself whether it isn't just as I say.

EUCLIO (*dumbly*)   I'm ruined! All these troubles on my poor
head, one after the other, a whole line of 'em stuck together! Well, I'll go in and find out how much of all this is
true. (*Goes into the house.*)

LYCONIDES (*calling after him*)   I'll be right in after you. (*To
the audience, happily*) Well, it looks as if I'm finally in safe
waters. (*Looking all around*) But I don't see my servant
Strobilus. I have no idea where he can be. The only thing I
can do is wait around here a little while, and follow the old
man in later. In the meantime, I'll be giving him a chance
to find out about my affair from the old woman who's the
girl's nurse. She knows the whole story.

(*As Lyconides looks off, stage right, Strobilus bursts in,
stage left.* [Act V traditionally begins here. To avoid interrupting the action I have not indicated it in the text.])

STROBILUS (*to the world at large, at the top of his lungs*)
God in heaven, what blessings you've showered on me! I
have a potful of gold—four pounds of it! Who's richer than
I am? Who in this city right now has more of heaven's
blessings than I?

LYCONIDES (*dryly*)   I think I heard somebody's voice coming from around here. (*He turns.*)

STROBILUS (*turning and seeing him*)   Is this my master I see?

LYCONIDES   Is this my servant I behold?

STROBILUS (*peering*)   That's who it is.

LYCONIDES (*peering*)   No one else.

STROBILUS (*walking toward him*)   I'll go up to him.

LYCONIDES (*walking toward him*)   I'll go meet him. I suppose he's been to see the old woman, the girl's nurse, as I told him to.

STROBILUS (*stopping; aside*)   Why don't I tell him I found this prize piece of plunder and then ask him to let me go free? I'll go right up and tell him. (*To Lyconides*) I found—

LYCONIDES (*interrupting, impatiently*)   You found what?

STROBILUS (*grinning*)   Not the kind of thing kids holler they find when they open up a bean.

LYCONIDES (*wearily*)   Having fun again as usual, eh? (*Turns as if to go.*)

STROBILUS (*hastily*)   Hey, wait! I'll tell you. Just listen.

LYCONIDES (*reluctantly stopping*)   All right, talk.

STROBILUS (*his eyes shining*)   Today I found a fortune!

LYCONIDES (*disinterestedly*)   Where?

STROBILUS (*ignoring the question, as before*)   A potful of gold, I tell you, four pounds of it!

LYCONIDES (*electrified*)   What's this you say you did?

STROBILUS (*chuckling and gesturing toward Euclio's house*) I stole it from old man Euclio here.

LYCONIDES   Where is this gold?

STROBILUS   In a chest at home. (*Importantly*) I want you to set me free now.

LYCONIDES (*roaring*)   I set you free? Criminal! Arch-criminal!

STROBILUS (*taken aback, but recovering swiftly and pretend-*

ing to be highly amused)   Come off it—I know your game. Good joke I just played to find out what was in your mind, wasn't it? You were getting all ready to take the pot away from me! What would you have done if I had *really* found one?

LYCONIDES (*grimly*)   You're not going to get away with that nonsense. Come on, hand over the money!

STROBILUS (*as if not believing his ears*)   I hand over the money?

LYCONIDES   Hand it over, I tell you, so I can hand it over (*gesturing toward Euclio's house*) to him.

STROBILUS (*as before*)   Money? From where?

LYCONIDES   The money you just now admitted was in the chest.

STROBILUS (*airily*)   Oh lord, you know the way I'm always blabbering a lot of nonsense.

LYCONIDES (*grimly*)   You know what's going to happen to you?

STROBILUS   I swear, you can kill me but you'll never get from me—

[The rest of the play is lost. From some ancient résumés of the plot that have survived, we know that Lyconides got Strobilus to return the money and that Euclio not only gave the boy permission to marry his daughter but threw in the pot of gold as her dowry.]

CASINA

DRAMATIS PERSONAE

OLYMPIO, *foreman of Lysidamus' farm in the country* (*slave*)

CHALINUS, *servant of Lysidamus on full-time duty as orderly for his son* (*slave*)

CLEOSTRATA, *wife of Lysidamus*

PARDALISCA, *her maid*

MYRRHINA, *wife of Alcesimus, and friend and neighbor of Cleostrata*

LYSIDAMUS, *an elderly gentleman*

ALCESIMUS, *an elderly gentleman, neighbor of Lysidamus*

A COOK

A PIPER

SERVANTS

SCENE

A street in Athens. Two houses front on it: Lysidamus' and Alcesimus'. The exit on stage left leads downtown, that on stage right to the country.

PROLOGUE

(*The speaker of the prologue enters, walks downstage, and addresses the audience.* [The prologue that follows was prepared for some revival put on perhaps three or four decades after the original performance. How much it preserves of the original version is hard to say.])

PROLOGUE (*bowing respectfully*) Greetings, good people who do honor to Honor—and to whom Honor does honor. (*Abruptly raising his head and eying them keenly*) If I've told the truth, please give me a clear sign to let me know right from the beginning that you're all my friends. (*Stops and waits for a round of applause.*)

In my opinion, the people who drink vintage wines are the wise ones—and that goes for the people who like to see vintage plays. Since you all enjoy old-fashioned things and old-fashioned writings, you ought by the same token to have a preference for old-fashioned theater. After all, the new plays coming out nowadays are worth even less than the new coins. Well, once the talk around town put us wise to your yen to see plays by Plautus, we decided to put on an old comedy of his, one you all liked—the old-timers among you, that is; I realize that the youngsters here don't know the piece, but we'll do our best to see to it they do. This play was the hit of the season when it first came out— and that was at a time when the flower of our playwrights were still living, the men who now have passed on to the place we all end up at. But, even though they're no longer with us, they can give us as much enjoyment as if they were.

I beg you, all of you, please give your kind attention to our actors. (*Gaily*) Anyone here worried about his creditors? Forget your debts, drive your cares from your mind. Today's a holiday: the finance companies are out having fun. Everything's quiet; peace profound pervades the financial district. Very logical, our finance companies:

during the holiday they won't dun any of you; once it's over, they won't pay any of you!

(*Stops for a moment, and then raises a hand commandingly for attention.*) If your ears are at leisure, will you please listen? I want to tell you the name of our play. In Greek it's called *Kleroumenoi*, in Latin *Sortientes*. Diphilus wrote it originally in Greek, and Plautus, the fellow with the name that barks, translated it later into Latin.[1]

(*Pointing to Lysidamus' house*) In here lives a married man well on in years. He has a grown son; the boy lives with his father in this same house. There's also a certain servant there who's flat on his back in bad health—correction, flat on his back in bed; I want to stick to the facts.

Well, the servant—now this goes back a good sixteen years—once saw, in the early light of dawn, a woman abandon an infant girl. He rushed up and asked her to let him have the child. She agreed. He carried it off, brought it straight home, gave it to the old fellow's wife, and asked her to take care of it and bring it up. And she did. She brought it up giving it every attention, exactly as she would have given a child of her own.

Once the girl reached an age to interest men, the old fellow fell madly in love with her. But, on the other hand, so did his son. And now, with neither of them knowing it, each is lining up his forces against the other, father against son. The father's commissioned the foreman of his farm to ask to marry the girl; the old boy has hopes, if it goes through, of setting up a love nest somewhere, behind his wife's back. The son's commissioned his orderly to ask to marry the girl; he figures, if it goes through, he'll have the object of his affections right in his own back yard.

The old fellow's wife discovered that her husband was involved in a love affair, and this put her on her son's side. Then the father found out that his son was in love with the

---

[1] Both titles mean "The Drawers of Lots"; apparently the play was dubbed *Casina* by later ages. For Diphilus, see p. xiv. "The name that barks," because *plautus* is the Latin for a breed of dog.

same girl he was and was standing in his way, so he packed the boy off abroad. But the wife saw through it, and she's looking after her son's interests even though he's not around. Now don't look for him to come back today during this play. He won't. Plautus didn't want it that way; he collapsed one of the bridges on the route.

(*Nodding knowingly*) I suppose some of you are saying to each other this very minute, "I ask you—what's going on here? Weddings between servants? Since when do slaves get engaged or get married? That's something new they've started, something you'll see nowhere on earth." Well, I tell you you will, in Greece, at Carthage, and right here in our own country, in Apulia. Why, there the slaves' weddings are usually even bigger affairs than the masters'! It's the truth, and I'll bet whoever is willing one bowl of good wine—providing the judge comes from Carthage, or even Greece, or, for my sake particularly, Apulia. Well? No one here to take me up? Oh, I get it—no one here feels like a drink.

But let me get back to that girl who was foundlingized, the one that that pair of slaves are yearning to marry. It's going to turn out that she's a respectable, freeborn Athenian girl. As a matter of fact, she'll behave like a thoroughly decent girl all through the play. But, believe me, once it's over, I suspect she'll be perfectly willing to play bride without benefit of clergy to whoever offers her the cash.

That's about it. Good-by and good luck, be brave and win all your battles just as you always have.

ACT I

(Enter Olympio, stage right, with Chalinus at his heels. Olympio is foreman of Lysidamus' farm, and his clothes, personal hygiene, and general demeanor make it immediately apparent that he is rather more at home on a manure pile than in a bridal bed. His name suggests the Olympian gods; by the same token we call a 250-pounder "Tiny."

The other is Lysidamus' son's orderly. Chalinus—the name means "bit" (of a bridle); an orderly doubles as groom, and this particular one eventually "bridles" Lysidamus—is the precise opposite of Olympio: immaculate, sophisticated, unmistakably a product of the city.)

OLYMPIO *(angrily)* Can't you leave me alone? Can't I say and think what I want about my own affairs without always having you around? What the devil are you following me for?

CHALINUS Because I made up my mind to. To follow you like a shadow wherever you go. So help me, even if you've got a mind to mount the gallows, I'm going along and that's that. So you can just figure from this whether you'll be able to pull any of your tricks on me and sneak Casina off to be your wife the way you're counting on.

OLYMPIO *(acting as if puzzled)* What business is it of yours what I do?

CHALINUS You've got a nerve! You just tell me what a two-bit hick like you is doing sneaking around town here.

OLYMPIO *(shrugging)* I feel like it.

CHALINUS *(contemptuously)* Why aren't you at your head-quarters—in the country. Why aren't you taking care of your official duties and keeping your nose out of things here in town? Back to the farm, you. Back to your domin-ions, Governor, straight back.

OLYMPIO *(loftily)* I haven't forgotten my responsibilities, Chalinus. I put someone in charge of the farm who'll take

good care while I'm away. I came to the city to ask if I
could marry that fellow slave of yours, that cutey beauty
Casina, the girl you're so madly in love with. And if I do,
once I take her off to the farm with me, I'll stay put in
my headquarters as still as a hen hatching eggs.

CHALINUS (*exploding*) *You* marry her? God damn it, you
can hang me till I'm dead before you'll ever get *her* in your
clutches.

OLYMPIO (*as before*) Then step right up and put the neck
in the noose. Because she's my baby.

CHALINUS Listen, you discard from the dung heap, she's
your baby, is she?

OLYMPIO (*smugly*) It's the truth. You'll find out.

CHALINUS Drop dead!

OLYMPIO (*gleefully*) The things I'm going to do to you at
my wedding! As sure as I'm alive, I'll make you miserable!

CHALINUS (*truculently*) And just what will you do to me?

OLYMPIO What will I do to you? I'll start off by having you
carry the torch for my new bride. Next, I'll hand you one
single jug, and point out eight casks, a copper basin, and
one single path to one single fountain. And if that basin
and those casks aren't full to the brim every minute of the
day, I'll fill that hide of yours full of welts. I'll have such
a beautiful crook in your spine from hauling water we'll
be able to use you for a yoke. Then, once we're out at the
farm, if you ask for something to eat, either you'll chomp
hay or you'll eat dirt like the worms—because, if you don't,
I'll have you hungrier than the patron saint of starvation
on a fast day! Last of all, when you're all fagged out and
famished, I'll see to it you get the rest you deserve during
the night.

CHALINUS What'll you do?

OLYMPIO I'll wedge you in the window where you can hear
me kiss her and hear her say, (*switching to falsetto*)
"Olympio, my darling, my honey, my joy, my life—sweet-
heart, let me kiss those sweet little eyes! Oh, you're so

lovely, let me love you to death, light of my life, dickey-bird, turtledove, bunnykins!" And, all the time she's talking like this, you, god damn you, will be stuck in the middle of the wall like a rat in its hole. (*Abruptly turning away*) And now, to keep you from getting ideas about answering me back, I'm going inside. I'm sick and tired of your talk. (*Stalks into Lysidamus' house.*)

CHALINUS (*grimly*)   And I'm following. Not a chance of your doing anything here without me around.

(*Chalinus hurries in after Olympio, and the stage is now empty.*)

ACT II

(*The door of Lysidamus' house opens revealing Cleostrata and Pardalisca. Cleostrata steps past, and Pardalisca waits on the threshold.*

Cleostrata, Lysidamus' wife and the benefactress of the foundling Casina, is a woman in her forties, whose look and manner reveal at a glance that she is no meek, simple hausfrau. Pardalisca, her maid, gives every indication of being an able assistant to a keen and able mistress.)

SONG

CLEOSTRATA (*through the doorway, to her servants inside*)
Now lock the cupboards and bring me the key.
I'm going to step across to see
My next door neighbor. Come and get
Me there, if my husband asks for me.

PARDALISCA (*handing her the key, surprised*)
He told us to get his dinner ready.

CLEOSTRATA (*grimly*)
Say no more! You run along. You can bet he
Will get no dinner today from *me*.
That living disgrace! He's out to defy
Both me and his son, just to satisfy
That lust of his. But I'll make him pay.
I'll even the score with that old roué—
No food or drink,
Just fag and nag;
I'll dish it out
Till I see him gag.
It's going to be
Exactly the life
He deserves, and he
Can thank his wife!
That oversexed antiquity!
That cesspool of iniquity!

(*Pardalisca disappears inside, and Cleostrata turns and starts walking toward Alcesimus' house.*)

> Well, now I'll go to weep upon
> My neighbor's shoulder. Oh, dear!
> Her door's just opened and she's coming out—
> Bad time I picked to come here!

(*Out of the house steps Myrrhina, Alcesimus' wife, a woman the same age as Cleostrata and dressed much like her. Once over the threshold, she turns to call to her servants inside.*)

MYRRHINA (*through the doorway*)

> Now I'm going next door, so you follow this way.[2]
> Listen, you! Doesn't anyone hear what I say?
> I'll be there if my husband or someone should call.

(*Muttering to herself as she waits impatiently*)

> When alone in the house, I'm so drowsy things fall
> From my hands.

(*Calling through the doorway in exasperation*)

> I told you to bring me out here
> The big strainer.

CLEOSTRATA (*calling*)

> Oh, Myrrhina!

MYRRHINA (*in pleased surprise*)

> Cleostrata, dear!

(*Switching suddenly to a tone of concern*)

> You poor thing! What's the matter? You're looking so sad!

CLEOSTRATA (*bitterly*)

> I'm like any poor woman whose marriage went bad.
> It's nothing but trouble whatever you do.
> That's why I was headed this way. To see you.

MYRRHINA

> And *I* was about to come over to you.

[2] It was infra dig for a matron to be on the streets alone, even just to cross to visit a neighbor.

What's the trouble? What's got you so heartsick this
    time?

Any trouble of yours is a trouble of mine.

CLEOSTRATA (*impulsively kissing her*)

    I believe you, I do! There's no friend I love more—
    And no friend that deserves it as much. I'd adore
    To be like you in so many ways!

MYRRHINA (*kissing her*)

                    You're a dear.

    Now I want to be told all your troubles, you hear?

CLEOSTRATA (*sobbing*)

    My husband's disgraced me. The worst *possible* way!

MYRRHINA (*looking blank*)

    I don't get it.

CLEOSTRATA (*surprised*)

          Get what?

MYRRHINA

                May I ask you to say
    It again? It's a complaint that I can't get quite clear.

CLEOSTRATA (*slowly and bitterly*)

        My husband's disgraced me
        The worst way that he could,
        And I'm left with no right
        To claim rights that I should.

MYRRHINA

        Very strange if it's so,
        Since in most of our lives
        It's the husbands who can't
        Claim their rights from the wives!

CLEOSTRATA

        Why, he wants to walk off
        With my sweet little maid!
        And she's mine! It was I
        Who raised her and paid

All expenses. He says
That he wants her as bride
For his foreman. But *he*
Wants to sleep at her side!

MYRRHINA (*whispering worriedly*)
  Don't say such things!

CLEOSTRATA (*looking around and shrugging*)
                    We're safe here now. It's just we two.

MYRRHINA

                                        That's so.

  (*Overcome by curiosity*)

  But how did you ever get that girl? It's hardly *comme il
    faut—*
  A wife, behind her husband's back, having money of her
    own!
  And if she has, she never got it by methods I'd condone:
  By stealing from the household cash or acting like our
    whores.
  It's my opinion that all you have is your husband's, dear,
    not yours.

CLEOSTRATA (*shocked*)
  And you're my friend! From all you've said, you'd think
    we're enemies!

MYRRHINA (*confidentially*)
  Be quiet, silly, and listen to me. Don't go against him,
    please!
  Let him do what he likes, let him have his affair.

  (*Smiling knowingly*)

                          You lack for nothing, you know.

CLEOSTRATA (*aghast*)
  You'd argue against your own best interests? Your mind's
    beginning to go!

MYRRHINA (*sharply*)
  Now don't be stupid!

  (*Waggling a warning finger*)

                Don't ever let, in all your intercourse,
  Your husband say a certain phrase.

CLEOSTRATA

                      What's that?

MYRRHINA

                            "I'm suing for divorce."

CLEOSTRATA (*in a tone of alarm*)
  Hush up!

MYRRHINA

          What's up?

CLEOSTRATA (*pointing to the wings, stage left*)
            Just look over there.

MYRRHINA

                        Well, who do you think you see?

CLEOSTRATA
  My husband. Look! You'd better go. Quick inside, my dear.

MYRRHINA

                                    I agree.

CLEOSTRATA

              As soon as we have some time,
                  Both you and I,
              I'll talk to you again—
                  But now, good-by!

MYRRHINA
  Good-by!

(*Myrrhina dashes into her house and Cleostrata moves off
to the side.*

*A second later Lysidamus enters. He is a spry old fellow,
feeble enough to have to lean on a stick but determined to
show as few signs of age as possible: his gray hair is pomaded
and curled, he is dressed as flashily as a teenage dandy, and,
from the look in his eye, no young girl could possibly pass*

He scuttles downstage and, without noticing his wife, addresses the audience.)

LYSIDAMUS *(gaily)*

My feeling is that love outdoes almost every pleasing
    pleasure.

There's nothing I can mention which can offer such a
    measure

Of the charm and spice of life. I wonder at our chefs'
    devices

To season food—they never use the best of all the spices!

A dash of love, and a dish, I feel, will satisfy any eater.

But leave out love, and it's flat, it gets no sourer or sweeter.

Why, love will turn bitter gall to honey, a sourpuss mild
    and mellow.

I base all this on what happened to me, not on talk from
    any fellow.

*(Ostentatiously smoothing his hair and adjusting his
clothes)*

The more I'm smitten with Casina's charms, the better
    grows my humor:

I'm a snappier dish than a fashion plate, a trial to every
    perfumer.

Whenever I find a nice perfume, I smear it till I'm reeking

To stir her passions—*(leering)* and, I think, I've got what
    I've been seeking.

(The leer suddenly fades and Lysidamus visibly droops.)

But my greatest torment is my wife.

The way that woman clings to life!

*(Shakes his head mournfully—and does a double take as he
catches sight of Cleostrata.)*

Why, there she is! And no picture of joy.

Better butter the old bitch up, old boy!

(Goes up to her and starts to put his arm about her.)

Well, how's my darling wife today?

CLEOSTRATA *(between her teeth)*

LYSIDAMUS (*still holding her by the hand*)
                I wish my darling Juno were
                More happy to see her Jupiter.

    (*As Cleostrata tries to twist from his grasp*)
                Hey, where are you going?

CLEOSTRATA (*twisting free and stepping away*)
                                        You let me go!

LYSIDAMUS

                Hey, wait!

CLEOSTRATA

                        I will not.

LYSIDAMUS (*like a coy lover*)
                                    I'll follow, you know.

CLEOSTRATA (*stopping and eying him distastefully*)
                Are you mad?

LYSIDAMUS (*passionately*)
                        Yes. Mad with love for you.

CLEOSTRATA (*acidly*)
                Well, *I* would rather do without it.

LYSIDAMUS (*his hand over his heart*)
                There's nothing can be done about it!

CLEOSTRATA (*exasperated*)
                You'll be the death of me, someday.

LYSIDAMUS (*under his breath*)
                How I hope and pray for what you say!

CLEOSTRATA (*overhearing*)
            Now *that* I'll believe!

LYSIDAMUS (*abjectly, as she turns away*)
                            Turn around, ma chérie!

CLEOSTRATA (*witheringly*)
            I'm as much your chérie as you're mine, believe me.

    (*Sniffing*)
            And from whence comes this smell of perfume, eh,
            chéri?

LYSIDAMUS (*clapping a hand to his brow, aside*)
Oh, my god! I'm a goner! She's got me red-handed!

(*Starts inching away unobtrusively*)
Now to wipe off my head with my coat's what's demanded.
God damn that perfumer who sold me this stuff!

CLEOSTRATA (*hauling him back*)
Why, you white-bearded worthless old weasel! Enough!
I can hardly hold in certain things I should tell you.
A creature your age to parade with that smell you
Have on through the streets! You old lecher!

LYSIDAMUS (*lamely*)

But I
Was just helping a friend buy perfume.

CLEOSTRATA (*to the world at large*)

Hear him lie?
And how quickly he does it!

(*To Lysidamus, with biting contempt*)
Simply *no* sense of shame!

LYSIDAMUS (*eagerly*)
But I'll get some. All you want.

CLEOSTRATA (*as before*)

You've been wallowing in sin
At the brothels. Which ones?

LYSIDAMUS (*promptly*)

You mean me? never been
To one.

CLEOSTRATA
Yes? I know more than you think!

LYSIDAMUS (*nervously*)

Is that so?
Tell me what.

CLEOSTRATA (*with arms on hips, and her nose against his*)
In your dotage you've fallen so low
Not another old geezer could possibly come

Within range, no not one. Well, where were you, you
 bum?

Where's the dive you were at, where you whored and
 got tight?

Oh, you're soused! Why, just look at those clothes!
 They're a sight!

LYSIDAMUS (*hand on heart*)

 May the lord strike the both of us dead if I've touched
    One drop of the stuff today.

CLEOSTRATA (*in a tone of finality*)

 Oh, go do what you like. Go gorge and get drunk.
    Go throw all your money away.

LYSIDAMUS (*giving up his act*) Enough, woman! Shut your
mouth. You've got my ears ringing. Save a little breath for
arguing with me tomorrow. (*Switching to a tone of lordly
authority*) What about it? Have you learned to control
your temper? To see that you do what your husband wants
done and not go against him?

CLEOSTRATA (*curtly*) What about what?

LYSIDAMUS What a question! About your maid Casina.
About letting her marry a fine fellow like our foreman and
be where she'll have plenty of firewood, food, hot water,
clothes, and can bear children and bring them up. And *not*
letting her marry that worthless good-for-nothing of an orderly who to this day hasn't managed to put aside a
plugged nickel.

CLEOSTRATA (*icily*) It's incredible how, at your time of life,
you still forget to stick to your own business.

LYSIDAMUS What do you mean?

CLEOSTRATA If you did things the right way and the best
way, you'd let *me* care for the maids, since they're in my
care.

LYSIDAMUS (*testily*) Why the devil do you want to give her
to that two-bit shield-hauler?

CLEOSTRATA (*loftily*) Because both of us should do what we can to help our only son. ·

LYSIDAMUS (*exasperated*) All right,. so he is my only son. But I'm as much his only father as he's my only son. He ought to give in to what I want rather than I give in to him.

CLEOSTRATA But you're up to no good, take my word for it. I smell it. I feel it.

LYSIDAMUS W-w-who? Me?

CLEOSTRATA Yes, you! What are you stuttering for? Just what *is* this that your heart's so set on?

LYSIDAMUS (*self-righteously*) To give the girl to a fine, decent servant rather than a good-for-nothing.

CLEOSTRATA Suppose I speak with our foreman and get him to agree, as a special favor to me, to let the other fellow marry her?

LYSIDAMUS And suppose *I* speak with the orderly and get *him* to agree to let the other fellow marry her? (*To himself, tight-lipped*) And I'm pretty sure he'll do what I ask.

CLEOSTRATA Agreed. Do you want me to. tell Chalinus for you to step out here? You put it to him, and I'll put it to the foreman.

LYSIDAMUS Fine with me.

CLEOSTRATA He'll be right out. Now we'll find out which of us is the smoother talker. (*She goes into the house.*)

LYSIDAMUS (*the minute the door closes behind her*) Finally I can say what I like: (*at the top of his lungs*) god damn that woman to hell and gone! (*Shaking his head mournfully*) Here I am in the tortures of love—and she's putting obstacles in my way! And it looks as if it's all on purpose. She's got wind of what I'm trying to fix up. (*The door opens and Chalinus steps out.*) That's why she's helping that orderly—it's on purpose, god damn him, GOD DAMN—

CHALINUS YOU— (*in normal tones*) wanted to see me, your wife said.

LYSIDAMUS (*tight-lipped*)   Yes, I wanted to see you.

CHALINUS (*sauntering over toward him, insolently*)   What do you want to tell me? Say it.

LYSIDAMUS (*as before*)   The first thing I want is for you to look civil when you talk to me. It's downright stupid to frown at a man who's got you in his power. (*Chalinus wipes the frown off, and Lysidamus hangs a smile on.*) Well, up to now I've considered you a fine, upstanding fellow.

CHALINUS (*snickering*)   Oh, I know. And if that's the way you feel, why don't you set me free?

LYSIDAMUS (*beaming at him*)   Oh, I want to. But my wanting to do it won't do any good unless *you* do something to help.

CHALINUS (*suspiciously*)   Well, I'd just like to know what you want done.

LYSIDAMUS   Listen, I'll tell you. (*Taking him by the arm, confidentially*) I gave my word to our foreman that he could marry Casina.

CHALINUS   But your wife and son gave *me* their word.

LYSIDAMUS   I know. (*Eying him narrowly*) Would you rather be an unmarried free man or a married slave—all your life, both you and any children you have? It's up to you. Pick whichever side of the proposition you want.

CHALINUS (*shrugging*)   If I'm set free, I'll have to live at my own expense. Now I live at yours. (*Sticking his jaw out*) And about Casina—my mind's made up: I'm not giving her up to any man on earth.

(*They eye each other balefully in dead silence for a few seconds.*)

LYSIDAMUS (*as if suddenly making up his mind*)   Go inside and call my wife out here in front of the house this minute. And bring a jug of water with you and a pair of markers for lots.

CHALINUS (*amused*)   Not a bad idea.

LYSIDAMUS (*grimly*)   Damn it all, I'll put a spoke in your wheel one way or another. If I can't get anywhere by asking, at least we'll draw lots. That's the way I'll get even with you and those backers of yours.

CHALINUS (*grinning*)   But I'm going to win.

LYSIDAMUS (*roaring*)   Damn it all, you'll win a slow death by strangling, that's what you'll win.

CHALINUS (*smugly*)   Try all the tricks you want. She'll still marry me.

LYSIDAMUS, (*as before*)   Get out of my sight!

CHALINUS   Don't like my looks, eh? (*Shrugging*) I'll live. (*He stalks into the house.*)

LYSIDAMUS (*to the audience, moaning*)   What a poor devil I am! Is everything against me? Now I'm worried that that wife of mine will talk Olympio out of marrying Casina. And, if that happens, here's one old man it's all over with. But, if she doesn't talk him out of it, there's still a spark of hope in drawing lots. Then, if the draw lets me down, I'll set up a sword for a mattress and stretch out on it. (*The door opens and Olympio appears in the doorway.*) Sh, here comes Olympio. Couldn't have timed it better.

OLYMPIO (*through the doorway to Cleostrata inside, passionately*)   So help me, ma'am, I'd as soon have you put me in a hot oven and brown me till I'm the color of toast as say yes to what you're asking.

LYSIDAMUS (*to the audience*)   Saved! From what I can hear, there's still hope.

OLYMPIO (*loftily*)   How come you're trying to scare me with those threats of yours about freedom? Why, even if you and your son are against it, even if neither of you want it, even if both of you say no, I can still become free and it won't cost me a cent. (*The door slams in his face. He shrugs and walks downstage.*)

LYSIDAMUS   What's the matter, Olympio? Who were you arguing with?

OLYMPIO   Same one you always are.

LYSIDAMUS   My wife?

OLYMPIO   What do you mean, wife? You practically live like a professional hunter: spend twenty-four hours a day with a baying bitch.

LYSIDAMUS   What's she up to? What did she say to you?

OLYMPIO   She's pleading with me, she's begging me not to marry Casina.

LYSIDAMUS (*anxiously*)   And what did you say?

OLYMPIO   I said, if Jupiter himself asked for her, I still wouldn't give her up even to him.

LYSIDAMUS   God bless you!

OLYMPIO   She's boiling now. She's so mad at me she could burst.

LYSIDAMUS   And, boy, do I hope she does! Right in the middle.

OLYMPIO (*with an obscene gesture*)   If you were any good as a husband, that's where she would. (*Disgustedly*) I'm fed up with this love affair of yours. Your wife's against me, your son's against me, the whole household's against me.

LYSIDAMUS   What do you care? (*Tapping his breast importantly*) So long as Jupiter here is on your side, that's all you need, you can snap your fingers at that small fry.

OLYMPIO (*hotly*)   That's a lot of nonsense! You know yourself how fast flesh and blood Jupiters die off. Furthermore, Jupiter, when you die, and the throne passes to the small fry, would you mind telling me who's going to guard my back and shins and head?

LYSIDAMUS   Things will be better for you than you think—*if* we can fix it up so I get to sleep with Casina.

OLYMPIO (*shaking his head*)   Oh lord, I don't think there's a chance. Your wife's dead set against my getting her.

LYSIDAMUS (*grimly*)   What I'm going to do is this. I'm putting two lots in a jug, and you and Chalinus will hold a drawing. Here's my estimate of the situation: (*melodramatically*) we have to draw swords and fight it out!

OLYMPIO What if the drawing doesn't turn out the way you want?

LYSIDAMUS (*shuddering*) Don't say such things! I trust in god. We'll put our hope in heaven.

OLYMPIO (*witheringly*) You can't sell *me* that idea for a plugged nickel. Every man alive has faith in god, and yet I've seen an awful lot of the faithful fooled.

LYSIDAMUS (*putting his fingers to his lips*) Quiet a second!

OLYMPIO What's up?

LYSIDAMUS Look! Chalinus is coming out with the jug and lots. We'll be joining battle soon to fight it out!

(*Chalinus and Cleostrata come out of the house. Chalinus is holding, in one hand a deep and narrow-necked jug full of water, and in the other a pair of heavy markers. Lysidamus is not content merely to pick lots out of a hat; he intends a full-dress, official drawing in which the lots are plucked from the bottom of a jug of water.*)

CLEOSTRATA (*to Chalinus*) Tell me what my husband wants from me.

CHALINUS To see you going up in smoke in the city crematorium.

CLEOSTRATA I dare say he would.

CHALINUS I don't dare say. I know.

LYSIDAMUS (*to Olympio, gesturing toward Chalinus*) There are more experts in the family than I thought—I keep a professional mind reader in the house! What do you say we break camp and march out to meet them? Follow me. (*Walking up to them, affably*) Well, how are you two doing?

CHALINUS Here's everything you asked for: wife, jug, markers, and myself.

OLYMPIO (*sourly*) You're one item I could do without.

CHALINUS (*grinning*) I'll bet you feel that way. I'm your personal needler. I get under your skin. (*Contemptuously*) Stinker! You're so scared, you're starting to sweat.

LYSIDAMUS Shut up, Chalinus.

CHALINUS (*to Lysidamus, loftily, gesturing toward Olympio*) Why don't you take him in hand?

OLYMPIO (*to Lysidamus, making an obscene gesture*) No, him—he's the one who knows how to put it in hand.

LYSIDAMUS (*to Chalinus, pointing to the ground in front of him*) Put the jug down here and give me the lots. (*To the two servants*) Now pay attention. (*Turning away from them to Cleostrata; with gentle reproach*) You know, my dear, I still have the feeling I've had all along, that I can get you to agree to let me marry Casina.

CLEOSTRATA (*blankly*) Let her marry *you?*

LYSIDAMUS Of course, me. (*A light dawning*) No, no, no—I didn't mean that. I meant to say "me" but I said "him." As a matter of fact, all the time it was for me I wanted— (*throwing up his hands helplessly*) Oh my god! I'm saying things all wrong!

CLEOSTRATA (*eying him distastefully*) You certainly are. And doing them wrong too.

LYSIDAMUS (*frantically*) Him—no, me— (*stopping and almost visibly pulling himself together*) Ah, now I'm back on the right track.

CLEOSTRATA (*as before*) You get off it pretty often, believe me.

LYSIDAMUS (*reproachfully*) That always happens when a person wants something very badly. (*Gravely*) Now, Olympio and I recognize your rights, and we both beg you.

CLEOSTRATA For what?

LYSIDAMUS (*in dulcet tones*) I'll explain, honeybunch. We beg you to do our foreman here a favor in this Casina matter.

CLEOSTRATA (*promptly*) I will not. I wouldn't think of it.

LYSIDAMUS (*grimly*) In that case, the two of them will draw lots.

CLEOSTRATA (*shrugging*) Who's stopping them?

LYSIDAMUS (*pontifically*) My legal opinion is that legally this is the best and fairest way. If our side winds up with what we want, we'll be very happy. If not, we won't let it get us down. (*To Olympio*) Pick a lot and see what's written on it.

OLYMPIO (*taking one and looking it over*) Number one.

CHALINUS (*bursting out*) That's not fair! You let him get his before me!

LYSIDAMUS (*to Chalinus, handing him the other marker, icily*) Take this one, please.

CHALINUS (*sulkily*) Hand it over. (*Takes it, examines it for a second, then suddenly looks up*) Wait! I just thought of something. (*To Cleostrata, pointing to the jug*) Just see that there isn't still another one in there under the water.

LYSIDAMUS (*roaring*) You good-for-nothing, you think I'm like you?

CLEOSTRATA (*to Chalinus*) Don't worry, there isn't.

OLYMPIO (*looking upward, fervently*) O lord in heaven, I beg you, today give me—

CHALINUS (*interrupting*) —trouble. Lots of it.

OLYMPIO (*turning on him*) If you want my opinion, that's just what *you're* going to get. I know how much of a saint *you* are. (*Eying the marker Chalinus is holding*) Hey, just a minute. That lot there—is that made of poplar? Or pine?

CHALINUS (*belligerently*) What do you care?

OLYMPIO (*to Lysidamus*) I'm afraid that thing's going to float on top of the water.

LYSIDAMUS Good for you, Olympio. Keep an eye on it. (*Pointing to the jug*) Now both of you drop your lots in here. (*They do so.*) There we are. (*To Cleostrata*) Check them, dear.

OLYMPIO (*to Lysidamus, excitedly*) Don't trust her!

LYSIDAMUS   Don't worry.

OLYMPIO (*as before*)   I swear, if she touches them she'll put a hex on them.

LYSIDAMUS   Quiet, Olympio!

OLYMPIO (*grumbling*)   All right. (*Looking upward*) I pray to god—

CHALINUS (*interrupting*)   —to get a ball and chain today.

OLYMPIO (*ignoring him*)   —that I draw and win—

CHALINUS (*as before*)   —a hanging by the heels.

OLYMPIO (*turning on him*)   —and you a nose blow that'll send the eyes out of your head right through the nostrils!

CHALINUS (*unruffled*)   What are you scared of? By now it must be all ready for you—your noose, I mean.

OLYMPIO (*nervously*)   Ah, you don't stand a chance.

LYSIDAMUS (*shouting*)   Now pay attention, both of you.

OLYMPIO (*glaring at Chalinus*)   I'm quiet.

LYSIDAMUS (*to Cleostrata*)   Now, Cleostrata, so you won't have any suspicions or say I tried any tricks on you, I'm going to let you do the drawing yourself.

OLYMPIO (*groaning*)   You're ruining me!

CHALINUS (*gleefully*)   And helping me!

CLEOSTRATA (*to Lysidamus, icily*)   Thank you.

CHALINUS (*to Olympio*)   I pray to god your lot jumps out of the jug and runs away.

OLYMPIO   Oh yeah? Just because you're a jailbreaker, you want everybody to be like you?

CHALINUS   I'd like to see your lot do what they say once happened in Hercules' family: dissolve in the water while we're drawing.

OLYMPIO   Pretty soon I'll have your hide so warm from the whip, *you'll* dissolve.

LYSIDAMUS (*to Olympio, shouting*)   Come on now! Please!

OLYMPIO (*grumbling*)   If this jailbait here lets me.

LYSIDAMUS (*looking upward, fervently*)   O lord in heaven, give me luck today!

OLYMPIO (*following suit*)   Amen. And me too.

CHALINUS   Not you.

OLYMPIO   Yes, me, god damn it!

CHALINUS   No, *me*, god damn it!

CLEOSTRATA (*to Olympio, matter-of-factly, gesturing toward Chalinus*)   He's going to win, and it's going to make you miserable the rest of your days.

LYSIDAMUS (*to Olympio, pointing to Chalinus*)   Sock that so-and-so on the jaw! Come on, what are you waiting for!

CLEOSTRATA (*to Olympio*)   Watch your step! You keep your hands off him!

OLYMPIO (*to Lysidamus*)   Should I slap him or sock him?

LYSIDAMUS (*promptly*)   Take your pick.

OLYMPIO (*throwing a haymaker at Chalinus*)   Take that!

CLEOSTRATA (*to Olympio, hotly*)   How dare you touch that man!

OLYMPIO (*grinning*)   My Jupiter gave me orders.

CLEOSTRATA (*to Chalinus*)   Give it to him right back. Give him a sock on the jaw!

OLYMPIO (*as Chalinus gets to work on him*)   Help, Jupiter! He's punching me to pieces!

LYSIDAMUS (*to Chalinus, hotly*)   How dare you touch this man!

CHALINUS (*grinning*)   My Juno gave me orders.

LYSIDAMUS (*plucking Olympio out of the mêlée, acidly*)   We'll have to put up with it. My wife's giving the orders in the family even before I'm in the grave.

CLEOSTRATA (*to Lysidamus, gesturing toward Chalinus*)   He should have just as much right to speak his mind as (*gesturing contemptuously toward Olympio*) that one!

OLYMPIO (*grumbling*)   Why must he put the curse on my prayers?

LYSIDAMUS   Chalinus, I think you'd better watch your step or you're in for trouble.

CHALINUS (*nursing his jaw*)   Fine time to tell me! After my face has been pounded to a pulp.

LYSIDAMUS (*to Cleostrata*)   Now, dear, draw the lots. (*To the servants*) Pay attention, you two. (*Aside*) I'm so scared, I don't know where I'm at! This is awful! The way my heart's been jumping all along, I swear I've got a case of the palpitations. My chest's getting bruised from the pounding!

CLEOSTRATA (*plunging a hand in the jug*)   I've got one.

LYSIDAMUS   Pull it out.

CHALINUS (*to Olympio, grinning*)   Aren't you dead yet?

OLYMPIO (*to Cleostrata, nervously*)   Let me see. (*As she holds it up, at the top of his lungs*) It's mine!

CHALINUS (*dumb struck*)   Well, I'll be damned!

CLEOSTRATA (*showing the lot to Chalinus, sadly*)   You lost, Chalinus.

LYSIDAMUS (*to Olympio, jumping up and down in his excitement*)   God was on our side, Olympio! This is wonderful!

OLYMPIO (*to Lysidamus, but looking down his nose at Chalinus*)   It's all because I'm so devout. My whole family is.

LYSIDAMUS (*to Cleostrata, majestically*)   Inside, madam, and start the preparations for the wedding.

CLEOSTRATA (*impassively*)   Just as you say.

LYSIDAMUS (*impatiently*)   Don't you realize it's a long trip from here to the farm where he's going to take her?

CLEOSTRATA (*as before*)   I realize it.

LYSIDAMUS   Inside now. Even though you don't like any part of it, see that you take good care of everything.

CLEOSTRATA   Very well. (*She goes into the house.*)

LYSIDAMUS (*to Olympio*)   Let's go in too. We'll put the pressure on them to speed things up.

OLYMPIO   Who's holding you back? I'm not anxious for any

more conversation while (*gesturing contemptuously toward Chalinus*) he's around. (*He follows Lysidamus into the house.*)

CHALINUS (*to the audience, utterly deflated*) Why don't I go hang myself? No, I'd just go to a lot of trouble for nothing, and on top of the trouble, I'd be out the cost of a rope. Besides, I'd give joy and comfort to my enemies. (*Mournfully*) Anyway, I don't need to: I'm already a dead man. I lost the draw—Casina's going to marry the foreman.

(*Stomps up and down a few times, shaking his head bitterly. Then, with clenched fists*) Olympio's winning doesn't bother me as much as the way the old man had his heart set on keeping her from me and giving her to him. What a panic the old devil was in! The way he scurried around and then jumped for joy when Olympio won! (*Suddenly turns toward the door.*) Ah—I heard the door open. I'd better go off over here. (*Moves to an unobtrusive spot near the wall of the house.*) My kind and loving friends are coming out. I'll waylay them from ambush here.

(*Lysidamus and Olympio, who is now dressed in his Sunday best, come out of the house.*)

OLYMPIO (*snarling*) Just let him come to the farm. I'll send him back to the city loaded like a longshoreman.

LYSIDAMUS (*nodding approvingly*) That's the way to do it.

OLYMPIO (*as before*) I'll do it. I'll take care of it.

LYSIDAMUS If Chalinus had been around the house, I was going to send him out to do the shopping with you, and add one more misery to our opponent's load of gloom.

CHALINUS (*to the audience*) I'll play crab now and scuttle in reverse up to the wall here. I've got to catch what those two are saying. (*Bitterly*) One of them gets me down and the other one burns me up. (*Backs up to the wall of the house while Lysidamus and Olympio walk downstage.*) Here comes that stinking piece of whipbait, and he's all dressed up. I'm postponing my hanging. I've made up my mind to send him down to hell first!

OLYMPIO (*self-importantly*)   Quite an assistant I turned out to be for you today. I got you what you wanted most in the world. Today you'll have the object of your affections, and your wife won't know a thing.

LYSIDAMUS   Sh! (*Going close to Olympio and fluttering his eyes at him*) I swear, I can hardly keep my lips from planting a kiss on you for all you've done for me, darling.

CHALINUS (*aside*)   What's this "planting a kiss?" What's up? What's this "darling" business? By god, I think the old boy's out to put the foreskin to the foreman!

OLYMPIO   Hey, are you getting passionate about *me* now?

LYSIDAMUS (*passionately*)   More than about my own soul, so help me. How about my giving you a hug?

CHALINUS (*aside*)   A hug, eh?

OLYMPIO (*shrugging resignedly*)   All right.

LYSIDAMUS (*circling around to get behind Olympio, as before*)   Ah, to touch you is like honey to my lips!

OLYMPIO (*roaring as Lysidamus goes after him from the rear*)   Beat it, lover-boy! Off my back!

CHALINUS (*aside*)   So that's it! So that's why he made him foreman! When I bumped into the old goat the other day he wanted to make me major-domo on the same terms. Right on the doorstep.

OLYMPIO (*plaintively as he warily keeps his distance*)   I did everything you wanted today. I made you blissfully happy.

LYSIDAMUS (*trying to close in*)   And I'll take better care of you than of my own self till the end of my days.

CHALINUS (*aside, making an obscene gesture*)   If you ask me, these two are going to get all tied up with each other before the day is over. That old goat goes after any male beyond the age of puberty!

LYSIDAMUS (*giving up the chase; rapturously*)   I'll cover

Casina with kisses today. What a good time I'll have! And
my wife won't know a thing.

CHALINUS (*aside*)   Aha! Finally I'm on the right track. *He's*
the one who's crazy about Casina! (*Jubilantly*) I've got
'em!

LYSIDAMUS (*as before*)   I'm dying to take her in my arms
and kiss her this minute.

OLYMPIO (*testily*)   Let her get through the wedding first.
What the devil's your hurry?

LYSIDAMUS   I'm in love!

OLYMPIO (*shaking his head dubiously*)   I don't think it can
be done by today.

LYSIDAMUS (*sharply*)   Yes it can—that is, if you think you
can be freed by tomorrow.

CHALINUS (*aside*)   I've got to strain my ears for real now.
(*Gleefully*) I'm very neatly going to kill two birds with
one stone!

LYSIDAMUS (*confidentially, gesturing toward Alcesimus'
house*)   I've got a place all set next door here, at my
friend's house. I let him in on the whole story of my love
affair, and he said he'd fix up a place for me.

OLYMPIO   What about his wife? Where will she be?

LYSIDAMUS (*chuckling*)   I hit on a wonderful plan. My wife
will invite her to our house for the wedding, to stand by
and give her a hand and then spend the night with her. I
gave the orders, and she agreed to do it. So his wife will
spend the night (*pointing to his own door*) here, and I'll
arrange to get the husband out of the house. You'll take
your bride off to the farm—but the farm will be (*pointing
to Alcesimus' house*) here, at least until I've spent my
bridal night with Casina. Then, at the crack of dawn, you'll
carry her away to the country. Clever, eh?

OLYMPIO (*tapping his brow significantly*)   Brainy.

CHALINUS (*aside*)   Go on, scheme, you two smarties. You'll
smart for it, by god!

LYSIDAMUS   You know what I'd like you to do now?

OLYMPIO   Whatever you say.

LYSIDAMUS   (*handing him a purse*)   Here's money. Go do the shopping. Hurry! But be on your toes, mind you: get only tender morsels, since (*kissing his fingers*) *she's* such a tender morsel.

OLYMPIO   Right.

LYSIDAMUS   (*rapturously*)   Get squidlets, octopussies, clamkins—

CHALINUS   (*aside*)   Where are your brains? Lambkins!

LYSIDAMUS   (*as before*)   —sole—

CHALINUS   (*aside*)   Sole? Why not a boot—to kick you in the face with, you old goat!

OLYMPIO   How about some snapper?

LYSIDAMUS   What do we need it for? We've got my wife in the house. She's our snapper—she never shuts those jaws of hers.

OLYMPIO   (*importantly*)   When I'm on the spot, I can look over the fish display and decide what to buy.

LYSIDAMUS   Good idea. On your way. (*Olympio turns to go but Lysidamus grabs him and hauls him back.*) And don't economize—buy plenty. (*Lets him go.*) And now I've got to hold a meeting with my neighbor here to make sure he does what I asked him to do.

OLYMPIO   (*impatiently*)   Can I go now?

LYSIDAMUS   Yes.

(*Olympio races off, stage left, and Lysidamus hurries into Alcesimus' house. Chalinus leaves his hiding place and walks downstage.*)

CHALINUS   (*to the audience*)   Offer me my freedom three times over, and that still wouldn't stop me from cooking up trouble for these two today, plenty of it. Or from telling this whole story to the madam right now. I've caught the opposition in the act, red-handed! And if the madam will only do her job, the battle's ours. I'll beat that pair to the punch! Today's our lucky day: now the losers are the winners! I'll go inside and what (*gesturing toward Lysidamus inside the house*) our other cook cooked up, I'll cook over in a different way. The menu he prepared won't be prepared, and I'll have one prepared for which he's unprepared!

(*Chalinus ducks into Lysidamus' house and the stage is now empty.*)

ACT III

(*The door of Alcesimus' house opens, and Lysidamus comes out, tugging after him a respectable looking gentleman of about the same age, whose whole attitude reveals reluctance, harassment, and distaste. It is his neighbor, Alcesimus.*)

LYSIDAMUS (*dramatically*)   Now I'm going to find out if I behold friend or foe, Alcesimus. Now I'll have the proof positive, the decision decisive. (*Raising a warning hand as Alcesimus opens his mouth to speak*) And cut out the lectures on my love life. And cut out the (*mimicking the tones of moral outrage*) "A man of your age! With your gray hairs!" And the "You a married man!" routine, you can certainly cut that out!

ALCESIMUS (*eying him distastefully*)   I've seen people in love but never a case as bad as yours.

LYSIDAMUS (*ignoring this last remark, warningly*)   Get everybody out of the house, now.

ALCESIMUS (*testily*)   Damn it all, I decided to send the servants, all of them, male and female, over to your house.

LYSIDAMUS (*nodding approvingly*)   Shows you're using your sense with sense. (*Waggling a finger at him*) Just remember, though, the song the birdies sing: (*as if mimicking a bird call*) "With food, with food, with food." Pretend these servants of yours are marching to Sutrium.[3]

ALCESIMUS (*wearily*)   I'll remember.

LYSIDAMUS (*all affability again*)   That's it. Now you're showing sense—more sense than a censor. Take care of things. I'm going downtown. I'll be back right away.

ALCESIMUS (*acidly*)   Have a nice walk.

[3] A historic forced march of the Roman army during which each soldier had to report with his own provisions.

LYSIDAMUS Have your house learn some letters and numbers.

ALCESIMUS What do you mean?

LYSIDAMUS I want it to say M T 4 U when I get back.

ALCESIMUS Ugh! I could murder you. You and your jokes.

LYSIDAMUS (*chuckling*) What's the use of my carrying on a love affair if I can't be cute and crack jokes? (*Raising a warning finger*) Now don't get lost and make me go looking for you.

ALCESIMUS (*resignedly*) I won't leave the house.

(*Lysidamus hurries off, stage left, and Alcesimus goes into his house. A minute later Cleostrata emerges from her house.*)

CLEOSTRATA (*to the audience*) Well, what do you know! So that's why that husband of mine was begging me so hard to rush out and invite my neighbor over! He wanted everyone out of that house so he could bring Casina there. Well, I'm not issuing any invitations! I'm not giving those nasty old goats any chance to have the place to themselves. (*The door of Alcesimus' house opens.*) Ah! He's coming out, this pillar of society, this bulwark of the nation—this neighbor of mine who's supplying my husband with a place he can have to himself. Buy him for a pound of salt and you'd still be overpaying!

ALCESIMUS (*grumbling to himself as he comes out*) I don't understand it: no one's come yet to invite my wife next door. For hours now she's been waiting, all dressed up, to be invited over there. (*Noticing Cleostrata*) There's Cleostrata now. I suppose she's coming to get her. Hello, Cleostrata.

CLEOSTRATA Hello, Alcesimus. Where's your wife?

ALCESIMUS Inside. She's been waiting for you to come for her. Your husband begged me to let her go to your house to give you a hand. Shall I call her?

CLEOSTRATA (*casually*) Not if she's busy. Let her be.

ALCESIMUS (*quickly*) She's not busy.

CLEOSTRATA   Never mind. I don't want to bother her. I'll
see her some other time.

ALCESIMUS (*puzzled*)   Aren't you people getting ready for a
wedding at your house?

CLEOSTRATA   Yes. I'm making the arrangements.

ALCESIMUS (*as before*)   Well, don't you need help?

CLEOSTRATA (*elaborately casual*)   I have plenty right in the
house. I'll drop in on her when the wedding's over. Good-by
now. Give her my regards. (*Turns and walks leisurely toward her house.*)

ALCESIMUS (*to the audience, baffled*)   Now what do I do?
(*Bitterly*) Damn! That was a dirty trick I played, and all
because of that toothless, filthy old goat who got me into
this mess. Here I am promising my wife's help as if she
was some kitchen maid! That dirty liar tells me his wife
is coming to get her—and his wife tells me no, she doesn't
want her! By god, I wouldn't be a bit surprised if our lady
next door smells a rat. (*After a moment of thought*) On
the other hand, come to think of it, if she had any suspicions, she'd have put me through a cross-examination.
I'll go in now and (*indicating by a gesture his wife in the
house*) put that barge of mine back in her berth.

(*Alcesimus goes in. Cleostrata, having reached her doorway, turns and addresses the audience.*)

CLEOSTRATA   Well, I did a fine job of fooling him, all right.
The way those two poor devils are running around! What
I'd like, is to see that broken-down, good-for-nothing husband of mine come along so he can take his turn at being
fooled, now that I've dealt with this other one. I'd love to
stir up some trouble between those two. (*Her attention
caught, she looks toward the wings, stage left.*) Well, here
he comes. To look at that solemn face, you'd think he was
somebody decent!

(*Lysidamus stomps in, obviously in a foul temper.*)

LYSIDAMUS *(to the audience)* If you want my opinion, it's the height of stupidity for a man in love to go downtown on the very day the object of his affections is to be in his arms. That's what I was dumb enough to do. I wasted the whole day, standing around testifying for some relative of mine. *(Grinning maliciously)* As a matter of fact, he lost the case and I'm delighted: at least he got something out of my being a witness for him. I have a theory about witnesses, to wit, that you should first inquire and ascertain whether said witness has his wits about him, and if said witness turns out witless, send him home! *(Suddenly noticing Cleostrata)* There's my wife in front of the house! This is bad. I'm scared: unless she's deaf, she's heard what I said!

CLEOSTRATA *(aside)* I heard, all right, and you'll pay plenty for it!

LYSIDAMUS *(aside)* I'll go up to her. *(To Cleostrata, with a great show of heartiness)* How are you, light of my life?

CLEOSTRATA *(icily)* I've been waiting for you.

LYSIDAMUS *(as before)* Everything in order by now? *(Gesturing toward Alcesimus' house)* Have you had your neighbor brought over yet to give you a hand?

CLEOSTRATA I went to get her as you told me to. But that pal of yours, your best friend, blew up at her over something or other. When I came to get her, he said he wouldn't let her go.

LYSIDAMUS *(snarling)* That's your worst fault: you can't be nice to people.

CLEOSTRATA *(witheringly)* Why, dear, it's the chore of a whore, not a wife, to be nice to another woman's husband. You go get her yourself; there are things to do inside, and I want to take care of them, *(acidly)* dear.

LYSIDAMUS *(promptly)* You hurry along.

CLEOSTRATA All right. *(Aside)* I'll put the fear of god in him, all right. I'll have lover-boy here in a bad way before this day is done!

(*She goes into her house. At the same moment Alcesimus comes out of his.*)

ALCESIMUS (*to himself, grumbling*) I'll take a look and see if the fond lover has come back from downtown. The way that old mummy fooled my wife and me! (*Turning and noticing Lysidamus*) There he is, in front of his house. (*Calling*) Damn it all, I was just coming to see you.

LYSIDAMUS Damn it all, I was just coming to see *you*. Listen, you good-for-nothing, what did I tell you to do? What was it I begged you to do?

ALCESIMUS What's the matter?

LYSIDAMUS Fine job you did of getting everyone out of your house! Fine job you did of sending your wife over to my house! All because of you my big chance is gone, and I'm a goner.

ALCESIMUS (*hotly*) Oh yeah? Well, you can just go hang yourself. Didn't you tell me with your own lips that your wife would come to get my wife?

LYSIDAMUS (*hotly*) And *she* tells me she did—and that you said you wouldn't let her go.

ALCESIMUS Oh yeah? Well your wife told me herself that she didn't need her help.

LYSIDAMUS Oh yeah? Well my wife has just told me herself to go get her!

ALCESIMUS Oh yeah? Well, that doesn't cut any ice with me.

LYSIDAMUS Oh yeah? Well, you're just ruining my life!

ALCESIMUS Oh yeah? Well, that's just fine.

LYSIDAMUS Oh yeah? Well, I'll just stick around for a while.

ALCESIMUS Oh yeah? Well, what I'd like—

LYSIDAMUS (*interrupting*) Oh yeah—

ALCESIMUS (*ignoring the interruption*) —is to do you dirt.

LYSIDAMUS Oh yeah? Well, that's what *I'd* like to do. You're not going to have the last "Oh yeah" today.

ALCESIMUS Oh yeah? Well, (*shouting*) god damn you!

LYSIDAMUS (*between his teeth*)   Listen, are you going to send your wife out to me?

ALCESIMUS (*roaring*)   Take her and go to hell, all of you! You, she, your wife, *and* that girl friend of yours! (*The two glare at each other for a moment. Alcesimus throws up his hands in surrender.*) Go away and leave it to me. I'll send my wife over to yours right away through the back yard. (*He goes back into his house.*)

LYSIDAMUS (*calling to him, all smiles again*)   Now you're a real friend! (*To the audience, exasperated*) Did I start this affair on Friday the thirteenth? Did I commit a sin or something against Lady Venus? Here I am, madly in love, and all I get is delays! (*A piercing shriek suddenly is heard from his house.*) Hey! What's all the noise about in my house?

(*The door flies open, and Pardalisca bursts out, shrieking.*)

SONG

PARDALISCA (*to the audience, burlesquing the style of grand opera*)

     I'm ruined, lost, utterly undone by Fate!
     Horror has my heart, I tremble from head to toe,
     And where to seek and whom to supplicate
     For succor, safety, shelter, I do not know.
     Just now, inside, I saw strange things occur,
     A terrible daring, naked, unparalleled.
     Cleostrata beware! Stay away from her,
     I beg you, before she does you harm. She's held
     In anger's grip. And snatch that sword away
     From her! She's out of her senses, her mind's astray!

LYSIDAMUS (*aside*)

What frightened her to death just now, and made her run out this way?

(*Calling*)

Pardalisca!

PARDALISCA (*without turning around, as before*)
> Lost! Whence comes this sound that caught my
> ears, I pray?

LYSIDAMUS (*impatiently*)
You turn around and look at me!

PARDALISCA (*doing so—and bursting into tears*)
> Dear master!

LYSIDAMUS (*testily*)
> What's wrong with you?

What scared you?

PARDALISCA (*impassioned*)
> Lost!

LYSIDAMUS (*blankly*)
> You're lost? How's that?

PARDALISCA (*as before*)
> Yes, lost. And you are too.

LYSIDAMUS (*as before*)
I'm lost? How come?

PARDALISCA
> Alas for you!

LYSIDAMUS
> Let's make it *you*.

PARDALISCA (*launching into a fainting act*)
> I'm falling!

Please hold me up.

LYSIDAMUS (*holding her with obvious distaste*)
> Now *what's* going on? Speak up and quit the stalling.

PARDALISCA (*as before*)
Please hold me by the waist. Now take your coat and fan
my face.

LYSIDAMUS (*aside, as he obeys orders*)
Now what's this mean? It's got me scared—unless she's been
someplace

Where Bacchus juice was served up straight, and found it
too enthralling!

PARDALISCA (*faintly*)
  Now put your hands upon my ears.
LYSIDAMUS (*roaring*)

> Oh you go straight to hell!

  (*Grimly, raising his staff menacingly*)
> God damn your ears, waist, head—and you as well.
> Unless I hear from you, and hear it quick,
> What this is all about, with this here stick
> I'll bash in all your brains, you bitch. You'll see—
> By now you've fooled around enough with me.

PARDALISCA (*sobbing*)
  Dear master!
LYSIDAMUS (*mimicking her*)
> What now, dear maid?
PARDALISCA (*as before*)

> You're so mad, so upset!

LYSIDAMUS (*between his teeth*)
> You're ahead of yourself—you haven't heard anything
>   yet.

  (*Shouting*)
> What's the fuss all about? Talk—and *don't* make it long!
> That ruckus inside just before—what was wrong?

PARDALISCA
> Just listen, I'll tell you. Inside there, your maid
> Started carrying on just before. I'm afraid
> She behaved in the awfullest way that she could.
> She did what no well-bred Athenian should.

LYSIDAMUS (*nervously*)
> Did what?
PARDALISCA (*dramatically*)
> Fear binds my tongue—no words come out!
LYSIDAMUS (*wearily*)
> Can't I *please* find out from you what this is about?

PARDALISCA (*as if making a great effort*)

> That maid you thought your wife should make the
> > bride
> Of your foreman, inside this girl—

LYSIDAMUS (*interrupting anxiously*)

> > > Did what inside?

> Tell me what!

PARDALISCA

> > > —behaved like a mean and nasty wife.
> She's making threats against her husband's life—

LYSIDAMUS (*interrupting, incredulously*)

> What about his life?

PARDALISCA (*groaning*)

> > > Oh god!

LYSIDAMUS (*frantically*)

> > > > Speak up!

PARDALISCA (*playing the scene to the hilt*)

> > > > She's got

> A yen to end it. And that sword—

LYSIDAMUS (*interrupting, with a roar*)

> > > > That *what?*

PARDALISCA (*matter-of-factly*)

> That sword.

LYSIDAMUS

> > > What about that sword?

PARDALISCA

> It's in her hand.

LYSIDAMUS

> > > O lord
> In heaven! Why a sword?

PARDALISCA (*rapidly, with trembling voice*)

> > She's been chasing us all through the house,
> > > And she won't let a soul come near.
> > We all hide under bureaus and beds
> > > And don't *dare* say a word for fear!

LYSIDAMUS (*aside, clutching his hair*)
    I'm lost, I'm ruined!

  (*To Pardalisca*)

                        But what could have hit the girl
        So suddenly?

PARDALISCA

                        Her mind—it's in a whirl.

LYSIDAMUS (*throwing up his hands helplessly*)
    Who's ever had a fouler role to play?

PARDALISCA
    If you only knew the things she said today!

LYSIDAMUS (*nervously*)
    What was it she said? I'd like to know.

PARDALISCA

                                    You may.

  (*Solemnly*)

                    She swore an oath by heaven's might
                    To murder the man she sleeps with tonight.

LYSIDAMUS (*gulping*)
    What, murder *me*? That can't be true!

PARDALISCA (*all innocence*)
    Just what's this got to do with you?

LYSIDAMUS (*to himself, chagrined*)
    God damn!

PARDALISCA (*as before*)

                        Or you to do with her?

LYSIDAMUS (*with a sickly grin*)
        A slip of the tongue. I meant to—er—
        Say Olympio.

PARDALISCA (*aside*)
                        How very neat—
            Here's a man who knows how to fall on his feet!

LYSIDAMUS (*with a dismal attempt at casualness*)
        She's not been threatening *me*, has she?

PARDALISCA (*sternly*)
>   Why, you're the very enemy
>   She hates the most!

LYSIDAMUS (*agonized*)
>   But how's that so?

PARDALISCA (*shrugging*)
>   You gave her to Olympio.

(*Excitedly*)

>   Neither one of you gets one more day, so she said:
>   By tomorrow you both, plus herself, will be dead.
>   I've been sent here to tell you, to warn you—don't go
>   Anywhere near her.

LYSIDAMUS
>   I'm a goner!

PARDALISCA (*aside*)
>   And rightfully so.

LYSIDAMUS (*lugubriously*)
>   O god, what sugar daddy, present or past,
>   Is as miserable as I?

PARDALISCA (*to the audience, jubilantly*)
>   I'm pulling a fast
>   One on him. It's all a plot cooked up before
>   By Cleostrata and her friend who lives next door.
>   These things I've told him—simply a pack of lies;
>   That's why I'm here, to pull the wool over his eyes!

LYSIDAMUS (*worriedly*)
>   Hey, Pardalisca.

PARDALISCA
>   What?

LYSIDAMUS (*as before*)
>   I want to find out—

PARDALISCA (*not very encouragingly*)
>   Find out what?

LYSIDAMUS (*weakly*)

　　　　　　　There's something I want to ask you about.

PARDALISCA (*with a great show of impatience*)

　　Don't make me late.

LYSIDAMUS (*anguished*)

　　　　　　　Don't make me desolate!

(*Nervously*)

　　That sword—hasn't Casina put that sword down yet?

PARDALISCA (*promptly*)

　　No sir! And it's not just one, it's two.

LYSIDAMUS

　　　　　　　　　　　Why two?

PARDALISCA

　　She says one to slaughter your man, and the other you.

LYSIDAMUS (*clutching his hair*)

　　The deadest man alive, that's what I'll be!
　　The thing that's best for me to do, I see,
　　Is put on armor—

(*Suddenly getting an idea*)

　　　　　　　wait. My wife! I say,
　　Didn't she go up and take that sword away?

PARDALISCA

　　Oh, no one dares go near the girl.

LYSIDAMUS (*indignantly*)

　　　　　　　　　Then she

　　Should beg her.

PARDALISCA

　　　　　　　She did. But Casina stubbornly
　　Refuses to set it down until she knows
　　She's definitely not going to be Olympio's.

LYSIDAMUS (*roaring*)

　　God damn it, just because she feels that way,
　　Like it or not, she'll marry him today!
　　After all, why shouldn't I finish what I began
　　And make her marry me—oops, I mean my man.

PARDALISCA (*archly*)
> These slips—they're coming rather frequently.

LYSIDAMUS (*mimicking her tones of a few minutes ago*)
> Fear binds my tongue.

(*Seriously*)

>   Please give my wife this plea:
> To plead with the girl to put that sword away,
> So's I can get back inside my house today.

PARDALISCA
>   I'll tell her that.

LYSIDAMUS
>   You beg her, too.

PARDALISCA (*shrugging disinterestedly*)
>   I'll beg her, too.

LYSIDAMUS
>   But sweet as pie,
>   The way that I
>   Have seen you do.

(*Confidentially*)

>   Now, listen here. You pull this thing,
>   And your finger gets a golden ring;
>   There's also sandals in it for you,
>   And lots of other goodies, too.

PARDALISCA
>   I'll see what I can do.

LYSIDAMUS
>   And make the girl say yes.

PARDALISCA (*turning toward the door*)
>   I'm going now, unless
>   There's something more
>   You want me for.

LYSIDAMUS
>   You go ahead.
>   But do what I said!

(*Pardalisca disappears into the house. At the same moment, enter, stage left, Olympio followed by a cook and a small army of scullions lugging bundles.*)

> Look who's here! My associate, back with a stack
> Of supplies, plus an army of cooks at his back.

OLYMPIO (*to the cook, gesturing contemptuously at the file of assistants*)

> Don't you dare let these thorns break their ranks now,
> you crook.

COOK (*belligerently*)

> And just why are they thorns?

OLYMPIO

> In a flash they can hook
> Whatever they touch. Then just try to get free—
> In a flash, there's a slash. Anyplace they're to be,
> Anyplace they're to work at, the damage can go
> Up to double what's paid them.

COOK

> Yah-yah!

OLYMPIO (*catching sight of Lysidamus, draws himself up and, unused to such finery, tries to adjust the handsome coat he is wearing; to himself*)

> Ho-ho!
> Now to wrap this around me in style, *comme il faut,*
> And go up to the master just so.

LYSIDAMUS

> Well, hello,
> My good man.

OLYMPIO (*importantly*)

> That I am.

LYSIDAMUS (*jovially*)

> Tell me, how do you feel?

OLYMPIO (*eying the bundles longingly*)

> You're for love—and I'm hungry and all for a meal.

LYSIDAMUS (*reaching out to caress Olympio's pomaded hair*)
    You've come to me all prettied up—

OLYMPIO (*sternly, ducking and avoiding the hand*)
                                            There I balk!

LYSIDAMUS (*taken aback*)
    Now, wait—not so uppity, you.

OLYMPIO (*starting to walk away toward the door*)
                                            And your talk
    Simply stinks, stinks out loud.

LYSIDAMUS (*reaching out a hand again*)
                                    What's the matter with you?

OLYMPIO (*batting the hand away, and continuing to walk*)
    You!

LYSIDAMUS (*trying to keep up but falling behind*)
        Hey, stop!

OLYMPIO (*over his shoulder, disgustedly*)
                    Vous êtes pain in the derrière, vous.

LYSIDAMUS (*snarling*)
                What I'd like to give vous
                Is le whip, entendu?
                And unless you stand still
                I've a hunch that I will!

OLYMPIO (*stopping and throwing up his hands*)
                    Oh, mon dieu!
                    Can't you let me be,
                        And go away?
                    Do you want to see
                        Me puke today?

LYSIDAMUS (*as Olympio sets off again*)
                Wait!

OLYMPIO (*stopping and eying him glassily, with ineffable
    contempt*)
                    What did you say?
    (*To the file of cooks, like a king to his courtiers*)
                Who's this person, anyway?

LYSIDAMUS (*puzzled*)
> I'm the master.

OLYMPIO (*as before*)
>> Of who?

LYSIDAMUS (*as before*)
> Why, of you!

OLYMPIO (*with utter incredulity*)
>> I'm a slave?

LYSIDAMUS
> That's right. Mine.

OLYMPIO (*fixing him with a piercing glance*)
>> But you gave
> Me my freedom. It's true.
> You remember, don't you?

LYSIDAMUS (*reaching out a hand to stop him as he starts off again*)
> Wait a second.

OLYMPIO (*roaring*)
>> Let go!

(*Olympio glares at him. Lysidamus seems to wither up before that scorching glance.*)

LYSIDAMUS (*humbly*)
> I remember. I'm *your* slave.

OLYMPIO (*nodding approvingly*)
>> Bravo.

LYSIDAMUS (*as before*)
> O my master, protector, patron,
> Dear Olympio, pray do me one—

OLYMPIO (*interrupting, as before*)
> That's the way. Now you're using your brain.

LYSIDAMUS (*fulsomely*)
> I'm all yours.

OLYMPIO (*the lord of the manor again*)
>> Yes, but what do I gain
> By having a slave who's a knave?

LYSIDAMUS (*humbly*)
>Well, how soon could you have me remade?

OLYMPIO (*eying the bundles again*)
>Just as soon as the table is laid!

LYSIDAMUS (*pointing to the file of cooks*)
>Then get them all going.

OLYMPIO (*shouting to the cooks*)
>>Get moving! No shirking!
>On the double inside, on the double get working!
>I'll be here for a while. Now you make me a meal
>That a man can get drunk on. But a meal with appeal—
>Give me none of that pap that a Roman will eat.

(*Starts to follow the cooks in, but stops when he notices that Lysidamus is not budging.*)

>You're going to stay?

LYSIDAMUS (*grimly*)
>>Where I've planted these feet.

OLYMPIO
>What's there left that should keep you out here in the
>>street?

LYSIDAMUS (*excitedly*)
>>They tell me your bride
>>Has a sword there inside
>>For dispatching us two
>>Without further ado.

OLYMPIO (*with amused contempt*)
>>Well, we'll just let her have it. I know
>>>These damned dames, you see.
>>They just do things for fun. You come on
>>>In the house with me.

LYSIDAMUS
>>Damn it all, I'm afraid I'll get hurt.
>>>You go in, and hide:
>>Look around and check up on just what's
>>>Going on inside.

OLYMPIO (*dryly*)
> Your life is no dearer to you
>   Than is mine to me.
> So come on, will you!

LYSIDAMUS

>   Since you insist.
> (*Cautiously falling in in back of Olympio*)
>   I'm behind you, see?

(*The two enter the house, and the stage is now empty.*)

ACT IV

(Enter Pardalisca from Lysidamus' house.)

PARDALISCA *(to the audience, chuckling)* I'll bet even the Olympic games, or any games anywhere, can't supply as much sport as the sportive events now being held inside for the benefit of our old man and our foreman.

Everybody's madly busy in there, in every corner of the house. In the kitchen there's the old man raising a holler trying to hurry up the cooks: *(mimicking)* "Do something, will you! If you're going to serve anything, start serving! Hurry! Dinner should have been all cooked by now!" Then there's the foreman, who's parading around, scrubbed and polished, all in white and with a garland on his head. In the bedroom there are the two ladies, busy dressing up the orderly to palm him off instead of Casina as our foreman's bride. *(Giggling)* And they're doing a marvelous job of pretending they don't know a thing about what's going to happen. Then there are the cooks who are holding their end up with a marvelous job of seeing to it that the old man gets no dinner. They're tipping over the pots, letting the water put out the fire, doing exactly what the ladies asked them to. And the ladies are dying to get the old man out of the house without his dinner so they can be the only ones to fill their bellies. I know those two: trencherwomen both of them; they can stow the stuff away by the shipload. *(Turning around as a creak catches her attention)* There goes the door!

(Lysidamus comes out. He stops on the threshold to talk to Cleostrata and Myrrhina inside.)

LYSIDAMUS *(through the doorway, doing his best to sound casual)* I'm going to eat at the farm, dear. Why don't you two be smart and go ahead and have dinner anyway, as soon as it's ready? I want to escort the new bride and groom to the farm so there's no chance anyone will run off with her; (*importantly*) I know the dangerous types there are about. You two enjoy yourselves. Now hurry and send both of them out right away so we can get there while it's still light. I'll be back tomorrow, dear. I'll have my share of the banquet then.

PARDALISCA (*to the audience, triumphantly*)   There goes what I said would happen: the ladies are getting the old boy out of the house without any dinner in him.

(*Lysidamus turns, walks away from the door, and catches sight of Pardalisca.*)

LYSIDAMUS (*startled*)   What are you doing here?

PARDALISCA (*all innocence*)   I? On my way where your wife sent me.

LYSIDAMUS (*suspiciously*)   Is that so?

PARDALISCA (*as before*)   Oh yes, it's so.

LYSIDAMUS (*snarling*)   What are you spying here for?

PARDALISCA (*indignantly*)   I'm *not* spying!

LYSIDAMUS (*pointing to the door*)   Out of here! Inside everyone's rushing around, and you're loitering out here.

PARDALISCA (*scurrying toward the door*)   I'm going.

LYSIDAMUS   On your way! Out of here, you dirty good-for-nothing! (*To the audience*) Has she gone? (*Hearing the door slam, with a sigh of relief*) Now I can say what I want. (*Rapturously*) When a man's in love, he can be dying of hunger, yet he doesn't feel hungry. (*The door of his house swings open, and Olympio appears in the door-way.*) Ah, here he comes with a garland on his head and a torch in his hand—my ally, my associate, my cohusband, my foreman!

(*Olympio walks downstage. He is resplendent in his full wedding regalia. A flutist follows at his heels.*)

OLYMPIO (*to the flutist, gaily*)   Come on, piper, until they bring out my blushing bride, let's have a nice song. Let's flood the whole street with my wedding march!

OLYMPIO and LYSIDAMUS (*who joins in*)
> Here comes the bride,
> Here comes the bride!

LYSIDAMUS (*heartily*)   How're you doing, savior?

OLYMPIO (*abruptly dropping his gaiety, peevishly*)   I need saving—I'm damned hungry.

LYSIDAMUS   How about me? I'm lovesick!

OLYMPIO (*as before*)   Doesn't mean a damned thing. You can feed on love. Me, my stomach's been growling for hours.

LYSIDAMUS (*grumbling*)   What are those slowpokes being so slow about in there, anyway? The more I rush them, the slower things go. You'd think it was on purpose!

OLYMPIO (*brightly*)   Suppose I hit them with more of the wedding march? Maybe that'll hustle them out here.

LYSIDAMUS   Right. And I'll join you—we're both in this marriage together.

LYSIDAMUS and OLYMPIO (*bellowing*)
> Here comes the bride,
> Here comes the bride!

LYSIDAMUS (*agonized*)   God, this is killing me! I could sing the wedding march till I split a gut, but I'm not getting the chance (*leering*) to split a gut the way I want to!

OLYMPIO (*eying him distastefully*)   God, if you were a horse, we could never break you in.

LYSIDAMUS   How do you figure that?

OLYMPIO   The way you champ at the bit.

LYSIDAMUS (*leering*)   Ever try to mount me?

OLYMPIO   God forbid! (*Turning around as a creak catches his attention*) There goes the door. They're coming out!

LYSIDAMUS (*fervently*)   The good lord wants me saved!

(*Enter Cleostrata and Pardalisca leading Chalinus, who,*

heavily veiled and wearing a flowing wedding gown, makes a convincing enough female figure.)

CLEOSTRATA (*overhearing, sotto voce to Pardalisca*)   He's already gotten a whiff of Mr. Casina even from this distance!

SONG

PARDALISCA (*tenderly, as she guides the "bride" over the threshold*)

Step over the threshold with care, blushing bride.
Start such steps safe and sound, so you're sure
      To stand over your husband,
      To be stronger and never give in,
      To defeat him and so
      Be his conquering heroine!
Let your voice, your authority rule everywhere,
Let him load you with clothes, while *you* strip him bare,
    Pull the wool o'er his eyes night and day—
    Never, never forget this, I pray.

OLYMPIO (*sotto voce, snarling*)

Let her slip the least bit, and she'll pay for it double!

LYSIDAMUS (*agonized*)

You be quiet!

OLYMPIO

        I won't!

LYSIDAMUS (*as before*)

          Why not? What's the trouble?

OLYMPIO (*gesturing towards Pardalisca*)

Why, the bitch there will make her a bitch of a witch!

LYSIDAMUS (*clapping a hand over Olympio's mouth and hissing into his ear*)

You'll upset what's all set to go off with no hitch!
To undo all we've done—how they'd love such a switch!

PARDALISCA (*to Olympio, handing the bride to him and intoning solemnly*)

>   Now Olympio, since
>   You wish to be wed,
>   Please accept from our hands
>   This bride for your bed.

OLYMPIO (*truculently*)
> You plan to give her to me today? Then give!

LYSIDAMUS (*hustling off Pardalisca and Cleostrata*)
> Go back inside.

PARDALISCA (*over her shoulder as she is being hustled off*)
>   You will be sensitive
> And spare her virgin innocence, won't you?

OLYMPIO (*taking the bride by the hand, promptly*)
>   Good-by. Will do.

LYSIDAMUS (*continuing his hustling*)
>   Now move, you two.

CLEOSTRATA
>   And now, adieu!

(*Cleostrata and Pardalisca go into the house.*)

LYSIDAMUS
> My wife—has she gone?

OLYMPIO
>   Inside. Relax.

LYSIDAMUS
>   Yippee!
> Finally, once and for all, thank god, I'm free.
> (*To the bride, crooning*)
> My prettykins, honeykins, spring-blossomkins—

OLYMPIO (*menacingly*)
>   Hey you!
> Be smart and watch out or you'll end up black and
>   blue.
> She's mine!

LYSIDAMUS (*leering*)

> I know. First right of usage, though,
> Belongs to me.

OLYMPIO (*thrusting the torch at him*)

> Here, hold this torch.

LYSIDAMUS (*clamping an arm around the bride*)

> Oh, no.

I'm holding *this*.

(*Raising his eyes to heaven*)

> O Venus all-powerful, who
> By giving this, gives blessings galore, thank you!

(*Embracing the bride passionately*)

> Oh, que belle bodykins!

OLYMPIO (*shoving him away and taking over the embrace*)

> Oh, my sweet wifeykins!

(*Suddenly lets go with a roar and hops about holding one foot.*)

> Hey, what's going on?

LYSIDAMUS

> What happened?

OLYMPIO

> She plants
> A hoof on my foot like an elephant's!

LYSIDAMUS (*taking over the embrace*)

> Oh, quiet! Her bosom's soft as any cloud.

OLYMPIO (*again shoving Lysidamus away and taking over*)

> This little breast's so cute—

(*Suddenly grabbing his stomach*)

> for crying out loud!

LYSIDAMUS

> What's the matter?

OLYMPIO

> Right in the belly I got a slam.
> But not with an elbow—with a battering ram!

LYSIDAMUS (*contemptuously*)

You're handling her too roughly, don't you see?

(*Taking over*)

She's gentle with a gentle gent like me.

(*Suddenly flies backward and barely keeps from toppling over.*)

Ouch!

OLYMPIO

What happened?

LYSIDAMUS

This cutie's strong!
She laid me out—or just about.

OLYMPIO (*leering*)

I'd say she wants to *be* laid out.

LYSIDAMUS (*promptly*)

What's holding us up? Let's move along!

OLYMPIO (*to the bride, crooning*)

On your way, little sweet,
Move those sweet little feet.

(*The three disappear into Alcesimus' house and the stage is now empty.*)

ACT V

(Cleostrata, Myrrhina, and Pardalisca emerge from Lysida-mus' house, all three in high good humor.)

SONG

MYRRHINA

> Well, having been wined and dined so well inside,
> Let's step out here to watch the fun with the bride.
> I haven't laughed so much since god knows when,
> And I doubt I'll ever laugh as much again.

PARDALISCA *(giggling)*

> I'd love to know what Chalinus does in that room.
> The brand-new husband with his blushing groom!

MYRRHINA *(chuckling)*

> What playwright's ever contrived a trick as smart
> As the one that we've just worked—a work of art!

CLEOSTRATA

> Right now I'd like to see my old buck come out
> With his face bashed in. He is, without a doubt,
> The nastiest codger alive. Or do you presume
> The other's worse, the one who supplied the room?
> Pardalisca, I want you standing guard outside:
> Whoever you see come out, you take for a ride.

PARDALISCA *(giggling)*

> I always do. Delighted to do so now.

[A line has been lost here. This scene was mutilated in the archetype from which are derived the manuscripts we have, and there are frequent gaps where words, sometimes lines, are missing. In these spots I have rendered what is preserved in prose, marking the lacunae with suspension points.]

CLEOSTRATA *(to Pardalisca)*

> Keep an eye from here on all that goes on inside.

[A mutilated line follows in which Cleostrata has Myrrhina follow her to an unobtrusive spot off to the side.]

MYRRHINA (*nodding approvingly as she follows*)
>   And whatever you want to say to her
>   From there you're free to speak.

PARDALISCA (*to Myrrhina*)
>   Be quiet, will you, please?
>   Your door's begun to creak!

(*Cleostrata and Myrrhina take their stand off to the side, and Pardalisca hers near the door. A second later Olympio bursts out. He is half-naked and his face is bloody and swollen.*)

OLYMPIO (*to the audience, panic-stricken*)
>   I don't *know* where to flee or to hide, or just how
>   To disguise the disgrace I'm so dreading.
>   That's how awful a scandal it was that did in
>   The old codger and me at our wedding.
>   I'm afraid and ashamed, and the both of us are
>   In a most ridiculous position.

(*Clapping a hand to his brow*)

>   Am I soft in the head? I ashamed? This is strange—
>   Never felt up to now the condition!

(*Calming down and speaking more naturally*)

>   Take the trouble to listen as I tell you my tale—
>   It is well worth your trouble to hear it.
>   Both for telling and hearing, the mess I got in
>   Is so silly that nothing comes near it.
>   As soon as I had the new bride in the house
>   Right away to the bedroom I brought her.
>   It was darker than pitch. The old gent still en route,
>   "You lie down on the bed here," I order.

(*Excitedly*)

I lay her out, put a cushion under her, start the sweet nothings so that, before the old gent . . . I suddenly slowed up since . . . I keep looking over my shoulder to make

sure the old gent . . . to put her in the mood for the act,
I start by asking for a kiss . . .

> So I reach, but I miss her—
> Since she won't let me kiss her.

The more that I hurry, the keener I get
> To break ground in Casina's plot.
I've a yen to deprive the old gent of the job
> Before he arrives on the spot.
So I slam the door shut to minimize
> Any chance that he'll take me by surprise.

CLEOSTRATA (*to Pardalisca, sotto voce*)
> All ready? Go up to him now!

PARDALISCA (*to Olympio, archly*)
> Well, Olympio, where's the new frau?

OLYMPIO (*to the world at large, agonized*)
> I'm found out! God, this means my demise!

PARDALISCA (*dropping her archness for a tone of authority*)
> So don't bother to stall,
> Just confess and tell all.

(*Smirking*)

> How's it going inside?
> How's it go with the bride?
> How does Casina do?
> Being nice to you two?

OLYMPIO (*hanging his head*)
> I'm embarrassed to tell.

PARDALISCA (*dryly*)
> You began very well—
> Just continue from there.

OLYMPIO (*as before*)
> I'm embarrassed, I swear!

PARDALISCA   Don't be afraid . . . I want you to start with
what happened after you got into bed . . .

OLYMPIO   . . . it's shocking.

PARDALISCA (*grinning*)   It'll be a lesson to our hearers . . .

OLYMPIO (*groaning*)   . . . I'm a goner!

PARDALISCA (*as before*)   Go on!

OLYMPIO   When . . .

PARDALISCA   What?

OLYMPIO   Wow!

PARDALISCA   What!

OLYMPIO   Whew!

PARDALISCA   . . . is it?

OLYMPIO   Oh, it was enormous! I was afraid she had [that sword], so I began to investigate . . .

> And while I'm feeling around to see if she
> Has got a sword, I grab this hilt, you see.

(*Scratching his head in perplexity*)

> But come to think of it, I could have told:
> If that was any sword, it would have felt cold.

PARDALISCA

> Go on.

OLYMPIO (*hanging his head*)
>   I'm embarrassed.

PARDALISCA (*as if struck with inspiration*)
>   Wait—I think I know:

> A carrot?

OLYMPIO

>   No.

PARDALISCA

>   Cucumber?

OLYMPIO (*pondering the question*)
>   I don't think so.
> I'll swear it wasn't a vegetable. Although,
> If it was, whatever kind it was, the blight
> Never touched the thing, it had grown to such a height.

PARDALISCA
What finally happened?

OLYMPIO
I speak to her and say,
"Please, wifeykins, why spurn your husband this way?
Because I wanted it to be just me and you,
Do I deserve these things you're trying to do?"
Without a word, she pulls her robe to bar
That part that makes you women what you are.
When I see that the promised land has been ruled out,
I ask permission to try the alternate route . . .

I want, in order to turn . . . She doesn't make a sound
. . . I get up . . .

MYRRHINA (*sotto voce to Cleostrata*) Marvelous story he's
telling . . .

OLYMPIO A kiss . . . And a beard like a set of bristles digs
into my lips . . .
The minute I lift myself to my knees, she pokes her feet in
my chest.
Down I go from the bed. She leaps on me and pounds my
face with zest.
So without a word and dressed as you see, I quit and run
outside,
Since I want the old gent to have a taste of the medicine
I've just tried!

PARDALISCA
Very good. But what did you do with your coat?

OLYMPIO
I left it in the room.

PARDALISCA (*gleefully*)
Well, what do you think of the trick we played? Pretty
good?

OLYMPIO (*gloomily*)
We earned our doom.

(*Suddenly raising his head and starting to tremble*)

Hey wait—a creak at the door. Oh, god! Is it *she* coming
after the groom!

(*Lysidamus comes out of the house, like Olympio in rather
bad shape: he has no coat or stick, his erstwhile pomaded
hair is disheveled, and his whole appearance is evidence that
Chalinus has done his work well.*)

LYSIDAMUS (*to the audience*)

I'm burning with shame through and through.
Things are such, I've no clue what to do
Or how to face up to my wife—
I'm that near to the end of my life!
All my sins are now known, so, poor me,
I'm a goner, I'm done for, fini!

. . . have me by the throat . . . how I can clear myself
with my wife . . . a coatless poor devil, that's what I am
. . . secret marriage . . . I figure . . . the best thing for
me . . .

I'll go in to my wife, and I'll bare her my back
To atone for this injury.
Is there anyone here, any man who would like
To take over the duty for me?
I've no clue what to do—except to do like
A bad slave, and take off through the gate.
To go back in the house means the end of all hope
That my back will escape its sad fate.
You can smile at such talk, but a beating, though earned,
Is something I'd hardly enjoy.

(*As he heads off, stage right, the door of Alcesimus' house
opens.*)

So I'll take to my heels and get going this way—

CHALINUS (*calling from the doorway*)

Hey, stand where you are, lover-boy!

(*Lysidamus stops dead in his tracks. Chalinus, still in costume except for the veil, and holding Lysidamus' stick and
coat, walks downstage.*)

LYSIDAMUS (*to himself, groaning*) Someone's calling me back—I'm done for! I'll make believe I didn't hear him and keep going.

CHALINUS (*running about the stage as if searching for Lysidamus; shouting*) Where's the man who thinks he can live like a Marseilles degenerate? You can mount me right now if you want, it's a perfect opportunity. Just step back into the bedroom. (*Coming to a stop across his path*) Now you're done for, damn it all! Come on over here; (*brandishing Lysidamus' stick*) no need to go to court—here's an honest judge I can haul you before.

LYSIDAMUS (*to himself*) Oh, my god, he'll crack my shins to splinters with that club! (*Doing an about-face*) I've got to go this way; that other road's a real shincracker!

(*Lysidamus starts heading toward the wings, stage left— and discovers Cleostrata barring his path.*)

CLEOSTRATA (*with amused contempt*) Well, hello, lover-boy.

LYSIDAMUS (*to the audience*) Look at that—now my wife's blocking the road! I'm between the devil and the deep blue sea, I don't know which way to run. On one side the wolves, on the other the bitches baying. And *this* wolf at the door carries a club. I guess I'll be making a change in the old proverb right now—and (*going toward his wife*) I hope I'll do better with a bitch at the door!

CLEOSTRATA Well, how are things, Double-hubby? (*With mock concern*) Why, Lysidamus, where are you going in this get-up? What did you do with your stick and the coat you were wearing?

PARDALISCA (*tartly*) Lost them in lechery while seducing Casina, if you ask me.

LYSIDAMUS (*aside*) I'm done for!

CHALINUS (*in falsetto*) Let's go to bed, you and I. I'm Casina.

LYSIDAMUS (*venomously*) You go to hell!

CHALINUS (*in falsetto, with mock reproach*)   Don't you love me?

CLEOSTRATA (*to Lysidamus, sharply*)   Answer me—what happened to your coat?

LYSIDAMUS (*nervously*)   Why, my dear, Bacchus' lady worshipers—

CLEOSTRATA (*interrupting incredulously*)   Bacchus' lady worshipers?

LYSIDAMUS (*stubbornly starting again*)   Why, my dear, Bacchus' lady worshipers—

MYRRHINA (*to Cleostrata, interrupting contemptuously*)   That's nonsense, and he knows it. There aren't any more worshipers of Bacchus.[4]

LYSIDAMUS (*aside*)   I forgot that! (*Stubbornly*) Well, anyway, these lady worshipers of Bacchus—

CLEOSTRATA (*interrupting, grimly*)   What about them?

LYSIDAMUS (*mumbling*)   Well, if I can't get away with that one—

CLEOSTRATA (*interrupting, amused*)   You certainly are scared.

LYSIDAMUS (*putting on the indignation act*)   Who? Me? That's a lie!

CLEOSTRATA   Well, you're pale as a ghost.

[In the next seven lines, too mutilated to give any consecutive sense, apparently Olympio joins Cleostrata in jumping on the old man.]

OLYMPIO (*self-righteously*)   And he's brought shame and misery on me too, through these crimes of his.

LYSIDAMUS (*sotto voce to Olympio*)   Can't you shut up!

OLYMPIO (*in ringing tones*)   I will *not* shut up! After all, it was you who begged me, and as hard as you could, to ask to marry Casina just to help along your love affair.

---

[4] Probably a topical reference. In 186 B.C. a law had been passed banning the cult from Rome.

LYSIDAMUS (*with histrionic incredulity*)   I did that?

OLYMPIO (*with heavy sarcasm*)   No, it was Hector of Troy.

LYSIDAMUS (*between his teeth*)   Who'd have shut *you* up, all right. (*To Cleostrata and Myrrhina, defiantly*) You mean to say I did all these things you say I did?

CLEOSTRATA (*witheringly*)   What a question!

(*Cleostrata glares at him. Lysidamus tries to glare back but in a few seconds wilts and decides to forgo defense for unconditional surrender.*)

LYSIDAMUS (*abjectly*)   Well, if I did, I did wrong.

CLEOSTRATA (*as before, pointing to the house*)   Just go inside. I'll remind you where your memory's weak.

LYSIDAMUS (*quickly*)   Oh, I think I'd rather rely on what you two say. My dear wife, please forgive me this once. (*Turning to Myrrhina*) Myrrhina, you ask her. (*Turning back to Cleostrata*) If from now on I make love to Casina, or, let alone make love, just even show the symptoms—if I do anything like that from now on, you have my permission, dear, to string me up and flay my hide.

MYRRHINA (*smiling*)   I really think you should forgive him.

CLEOSTRATA (*to Myrrhina*)   If you say so, then I'll do it. (*To Lysidamus*) And there's another reason why I'm forgiving you and not being hard on you: this play is long enough; let's not make it any longer.

LYSIDAMUS (*timidly*)   You're not angry at me?

CLEOSTRATA   No, I'm not.

LYSIDAMUS   Can I believe it? On the level?

CLEOSTRATA   On the level.

LYSIDAMUS (*winking at the audience*)   There's not another man who has as nice a wife as I.

CLEOSTRATA (*to Chalinus*)   Give him back his coat and stick.

CHALINUS (*handing them over*)   Here they are, if you want them. (*In falsetto*) I was done wrong by, today, simply terribly! I was married to two husbands—and neither one gave me what a bride usually gets!

(*All enter Lysidamus' house, and the stage is now empty. A moment later, the speaker of the epilogue enters and addresses the audience.*)

EPILOGUE   Ladies and gentlemen, let me tell you what's going to happen inside: they'll find out that Casina is really the next door neighbor's daughter, and she'll marry Euthynicus, the son of the house.

   And now it's only proper that you pay us the prize of applause we've properly earned. Anyone who does, is to get the girl he wants without his wife ever hearing of it. Anyone who doesn't clap as loud as he can, is to mount a goat instead of a girl, and one perfumed like a privy at that!

CPSIA information can be obtained at www.ICGtesting.com
Printed in the USA
LVOW041508030113

314242LV00001B/73/P